"Biblical scholar Michelle Keener has t the song it sings, in the hands of this trauma survivor, is surprising and tender. It is a song of grief and loss expressed, of friendship that succeeds and fails, of a shattered world painfully reconstructed. Above all, this book sings of a Scripture that is sensitive to survivors of trauma, and a God who meets them in the ashes."

Helen Paynter, executive director of the Centre for the Study of Bible and Violence

"Michelle Keener has provided an excellent resource for those who want to become better stewards of other people's pain. Her research on trauma and the book of Job are insightful and invaluable. This book is instructive for individuals as well as church communities on how to deal with trauma in ways that promote healing."

May Young, associate professor of biblical studies at Taylor University

"Michelle Keener has given us all a gift to be treasured—whether we have experienced trauma or want to walk well with those who have. *Comfort in the Ashes* assists readers in understanding trauma and the healing process while offering a perceptive and illuminating reading of the book of Job. Reading Job through the lens of trauma recovery makes space for a healing encounter with God on the pages of Scripture. I'm personally grateful for the way this book taught and ministered to me, and I'm eager to share it with others!"

Carmen Joy Imes, associate professor of Old Testament at the Talbot School of Theology and author of *Bearing God's Name* and *Being God's Image*

"How can churches support those living in the wake of trauma? How do we love those with shattered lives well? Drawing on the latest psychological research into trauma, Michelle Keener provides a way forward that is deeply rooted in the biblical text. Based on extensive research and written with a compassion that comes only from experience, *Comfort in the Ashes* invites us to minister well to those with shattered lives, providing sanctuary, avoiding additional harm, and inviting their presence as beloved members of our communities."

Jennifer Brown Jones, professor of Old Testament at Liberty University

"For those who have ever asked, 'Why me?' or 'Where is God?' Michelle Keener offers a path forward in her trauma-informed reading of Job. Keener breaks new ground in biblical studies as she views Job's experiences through the lens of trauma theory. Keener's unflinching focus on hard questions and her multilayered research into trauma's impact make this book a must-read for pastors and scholars, as well as those impacted by trauma. *Comfort in the Ashes* provides practical steps for churches and individuals to create a safe environment for survivors to resolve their trauma and embrace a deeper understanding of God's comfort and care."

Lynn H. Cohick, distinguished professor of New Testament at Houston Christian University

MICHELLE K. KEENER

FOREWORD BY SCOT McKNIGHT

COMFORT

IN

THE

ASHES

EXPLORATIONS in the BOOK
of JOB to SUPPORT
TRAUMA SURVIVORS

ivp
Academic
An imprint of InterVarsity Press
Downers Grove, Illinois

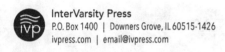

InterVarsity Press
P.O. Box 1400 | Downers Grove, IL 60515-1426
ivpress.com | email@ivpress.com

InterVarsity Press® is the publishing division of InterVarsity Christian Fellowship/USA®. For more information, visit intervarsity.org.

Scripture quotations, unless otherwise noted, are from the New Revised Standard Version, Updated Edition. Copyright © 2021 National Council of Churches of Christ in the United States of America. Used by permission. All rights reserved worldwide.

The publisher cannot verify the accuracy or functionality of website URLs used in this book beyond the date of publication.

Cover design: David Fassett
Interior design: Daniel van Loon
Images: Moment and Getty Images: © jayk7, © by Ruhey, © Matt Anderson Photography,
          © kampee patisena, © Yifei Fang

ISBN 978-1-5140-1034-1 (print) | ISBN 978-1-5140-1035-8 (digital)

Printed in the United States of America ∞

Library of Congress Cataloging-in-Publication Data
Names: Keener, Michelle, 1973- author.
Title: Comfort in the ashes : explorations in the book of Job to support
  trauma survivors / Michelle K. Keener.
Description: Downers Grove, IL : IVP Academic, [2025] | Includes
  bibliographical references and index.
Identifiers: LCCN 2024026706 (print) | LCCN 2024026707 (ebook) | ISBN
  9781514010341 (print) | ISBN 9781514010358 (digital)
Subjects: LCSH: Psychic trauma–Biblical teaching. | Bible. Job–Criticism,
  interpretation, etc. | BISAC: RELIGION / Christian Ministry / Counseling
  & Recovery | RELIGION / Christian Ministry / Pastoral Resources
Classification: LCC BS1199.P88 K33 2025 (print) | LCC BS1199.P88 (ebook)
  | DDC 259–dc23/eng/20240708
LC record available at https://lccn.loc.gov/2024026706
LC ebook record available at https://lccn.loc.gov/2024026707

32   31   30   29   28   27   26   25 | 13   12   11   10   9   8   7   6   5   4   3   2   1

DEDICATED *to*

CHRIS AND RONI EARLEY

Semper Fidelis

CONTENTS

FOREWORD

Scot McKnight

IT ONLY TAKES TWO SKILLS to agree with the core of Michelle Keener's book: (1) a basic understanding of trauma and (2) an empathic imagination. One cannot read Job's opening chapter and not feel the man's pain. It takes more than imagination not to think he was traumatized. Trauma is a response to an event, an experience, or a culture that overwhelms and threatens a person's identity, security, and safety. I like how Michelle says it: "Trauma is an event that goes beyond our ordinary capacity for coping and functioning. Trauma devastates. It dismantles." Trauma is defined a little more expansively by SAMHSA, when they say trauma results from "an event, series of events, or set of circumstances that is experienced by an individual as physically or emotionally harmful or life threatening and that has lasting adverse effects on the individual's functioning and mental, physical, social, emotional, or spiritual well-being."[1] Job fits the description. He was a trauma survivor.

We tend to idealize the Bible's heroic characters, like Abraham or Sarah, Moses, David, Jeremiah, Mary, Paul, and Peter. But a little empathic imagination about Sarah leads us to think that when Abraham foolishly handing her off when in Egypt, that must have traumatized her. David's own exile from power and potential must have led him not only to his knees in prayer but to that telltale sign of trauma: a feeling of being overwhelmed and threatened. Jeremiah wept and mourned

---

[1]Substance Abuse and Mental Health Services Administration. SAMHSA's Concept of Trauma and Guidance for a Trauma-Informed Approach. HHS publication number (SMA) 14-4884. Rockville, MD: Substance Abuse and Mental Health Services Administration, 2014.

and complained like someone who knows chronic trauma. I wonder how the rejections of Jesus Mary witnessed in Galilee and the bloody, humiliating crucifixion of her son affected her. What was life like for her from that fateful Friday evening to the first report of her son's resurrection? Surely she was overwhelmed and feared for her own safety. Paul's erratic words in the last few chapters of 2 Corinthians manifest the experience of trauma. I, too, wonder about Peter's reunion with the apostles between the evening of his betrayals and the vindication of his calling at Pentecost. One doesn't have to be a psychologist to at least wonder if these major figures were at times traumatized.

This is why Michelle Keener's study about Job is a wonderful example of what is hiding in plain sight for us all to see: Job's wordlessness and discourses, frustrations and stubbornness, not to mention his anger and vehemency, are boilerplate signs of trauma. Once we cross the threshold of the diagnosis, we simply can't let it go. Job becomes a real human with real experiences and real confusion and real crippling, traumatic feelings. We feel his sense that he's a victim and that he aches for justice. Telling his story over and over, as Job does, takes us into the therapist's office who knows clients will need to tell their story all over again. Trauma, Michelle reminds us all, is not our fault. It is our body's response to an experience that was too much for us. A tragic event—a death, a divorce, a disaster—can be experienced in different ways, but for some the tragedy is embodied in trauma. Trauma lurks in our body, and at times is triggered by a sound, a voice, a memory, a perception that the old threat has not left.

The church needs us to humanize the Bible's characters. They are like us far more than unlike us. Our trauma is theirs, and theirs can be ours. Michelle probes Job's life in a way that makes him far more like us than we might realize. His desire for order, his silences, his shocking turns of phrase, his irascibility and venting, his impatience with his friends, his shifts from one strategy to another, and his claims of righteousness sound so much like our yearnings for order and venting, silences, laments, shifts, choices of words, and ponderings of those who have been traumatized. Those insights of this book make the man come alive—for us. While Job leads our best thinkers to wonder their way into theodicies and the problem of evil, recognizing his trauma shifts from the theoretical and philosophical to the practical and the therapeutic. This is exactly what Michelle Keener offers us in this informed and valuable study. The original language of Job requires expertise and finesse to comprehend. That Michelle wrote her doctoral dissertation on this book provides for her readers a special treat: nuance in the poetry, in the prose, and in moments of transition. Welcome to the world of Job and his trauma.

ACKNOWLEDGMENTS

MAY WOUNDED HEARTS FIND refuge here.

That was the dedication on my dissertation when I first wrote about Job and trauma. I am more keenly aware now than ever before of how many people carry deep wounds and scars. It is my hope that those who are suffering, those who are carrying pain and loss, longing and sorrow, will find refuge in these pages. May you discover that you are not alone and the storm you're facing will not last forever.

It is also my fervent hope that this book will help churches recognize those who are suffering and reach out to support them. The church has an opportunity to bring words of healing and hope to people who desperately need to hear them.

I am so grateful for the people in my life who have spoken those words to me.

My deepest thanks go to Dr. Jennifer Brown Jones, not only my mentor and dissertation supervisor, but now my dear friend. None of this would have been possible without her brilliant insights and encouragement.

Extra special thanks to my pastors, Terry and Tracy Jimmerson. You gave me a church home when I needed one. You not only gave me a place to heal and serve, but you have shared your friendship with me as well. I am so grateful for you both.

Huge thanks to my editor Rachel Hastings for her tireless support and advocacy for this book, and for her endless supply of kindness, humor, and patience. Many thanks as well to the entire team at IVP Academic for believing in this project and bringing it to fruition.

As always, my family deserves more than a thank you. They have put up with Job and trauma for four years and yet still listen patiently when I talk about it. Thank you for your love. Thank you for cheering me on. Thank you for being my biggest champions and greatest supporters. And thank you for the chocolate. I love you all.

My sincere thanks to every person who has courageously and generously shared their story with me. I will hold those stories close and steward them well. May the God of peace surround you with His love and hold you close as you heal. People may have failed you, but God will not.

And above all, I thank and praise God for his faithfulness, his love, and his incredible grace. He truly does give beauty for ashes.

Soli Deo Gloria

INTRODUCTION

Trauma isn't just sadness on steroids. It is not stepping on a Lego twice or forgetting to record your favorite show. Trauma is an event that goes beyond our ordinary capacity for coping and functioning. Trauma devastates. It dismantles. It goes to the heart of our most deeply held beliefs about God, the world, and our place in it. It hits us at the very core of who we are and what we believe and leaves us forever changed.

And so often the church is unprepared for it.

I never intended to write a book about trauma and the Bible. When I started my PhD program, I wanted to research and write about discipleship, but when I walked through a season of intense personal suffering, I came face-to-face with trauma in all of its brutal, lonely, confusing pain. I don't recommend the experience, but the truth is, trauma and suffering are a part of the world we live in. No one is immune from wounding and sorrow—it finds us all. For many of us as New Testament believers, the church is where we turn for comfort, for support, for answers. When our world falls apart, we go to the church looking for the glue that will keep it together. We turn to our pastors and elders, our leaders, and our friends in the hope that they will have the words we need to hear. That somehow these men and women of God, men and women we trust, will know what to say to make it better. Unfortunately, many times the response that trauma survivors[1] receive from our church community makes things worse. Not because our leaders and friends are uncaring or unconcerned, but simply because most of us in the church are not prepared to deal with the reality of trauma and respond in a healthy, life-giving way.

As pastors, church leaders, and believers, we know we live in a broken world filled with broken people. And let's be honest, those of us who lead in the church can be just as wounded and broken as the people we minister to. We know hurt and loss and sorrow will come, and we are often prepared with neat and tidy Christian responses for when bad things happen. We have Bible verses at the ready to repeat when someone comes to us with a broken heart or a terrifying diagnosis. We rely on those verses because we believe them, and we know that God's promises are true. We know God restores and redeems. We know God forgives and comforts. We know God is with us in our darkest times. But in our hurry to provide a quick Christian answer, to rush people from sorrow to joy, to jump ahead to the happily ever after testimony that we believe is coming, we may be unintentionally making the situation worse. As counterintuitive as it may feel, sometimes we need to stop trying to provide an answer and provide our presence instead. For many of us, when we're in the midst of trauma and suffering we don't need a lecture on theology and we don't need answers we've heard a thousand times; we need to know we are not alone. When we're in the ashes of our trauma, we need someone who is willing to sit in the dirt with us.

We can see this play out in the book of Job. It is a story that has so much to teach all of us, survivors and comforters alike, about trauma.

---

[1]Throughout this book I will use the phrase *trauma survivors* to refer to those of us who have been through a trauma-inducing experience. I understand that this is only one of many phrases we can use to refer to people who have been through trauma, and there are some who may find this phrase an unwelcome or unhelpful label. None of us should be defined by only one moment in our lives. A trauma survivor is certainly more than just that one experience. I recognize that and respect it. I have chosen to use *trauma survivor* to honor all those who have suffered, myself included. It is my hope that if you have walked through, or are currently walking through, trauma that you will not see this terminology as a label I assign you, but instead as an encouragement that you are seen, valued, and respected.

Job was a righteous man. A man who did all the right things, who followed the rules, who lived his life well. He was a man with wealth, reputation, family, and a deep devotion to God. Then, one day, it's all ripped away. In a series of terrible calamities Job loses his children, his wealth, his reputation and status in the community, even his health. One loss after another piles up until he has nothing left. He is exiled to the town garbage dump, sitting in the ashes of shame, loss, and physical pain, his body covered with oozing sores, with no explanation for why this has happened. Why him? Why his children? Why his family? Why God?

Haven't we all been there at some point? Why God? Why me? Why now? Where are you? Please make it stop. Trauma upends our life, shatters everything we know about the world, and leaves us in chaos and confusion. And when we turn to the people we think have all the answers, when we turn to our church or to trusted Christian friends, we are all too often met with a pat on the back, a Bible verse, and a promise that they'll pray for us in their next quiet time moment. Or we're told to forgive and move on, to let go and let God, to stop dwelling on it and think of better things. We're expected to pick up the fragments of our life, wrap them in Bible verses, and get on with it.

But what if we can't?

What if the trauma is too big, too hard, too disorienting?

Left alone in our sorrow, we may start to wonder if the flaw is in us. Maybe my faith isn't strong enough. Maybe I did something wrong. Maybe God is mad at me. And down the road to a secondary trauma we go. The trauma of not being heard, of not being seen, of being brushed aside because our pain is too much. Because we are too much.

But here's the thing about trauma . . . it's not your fault. Maybe I should say that again. Trauma is not your fault. You are not weak or defective. Your faith is not too small, and your sin is not too great. Trauma is a category 5 hurricane and no amount of plywood on the windows can stop it. Trauma overwhelms our brains and our bodies in a way we can't control. That's what makes it trauma. If we could cope with it and figure it out and pick ourselves up and dust ourselves off without much work, it wouldn't be trauma. It might be sadness or grief or anger, but it's not trauma. Trauma breaks through our coping skills like a tidal wave crashing through a dam. There is no way to prepare for it, there is nothing you could have done. Trauma takes over. What we need is a church that knows how to recognize the signs of trauma and how to respond to it in a way that leads to healing, not more wounding. I've experienced that kind of wounding by the people I turned to for help. Maybe you have too. And if you have, I'm sorry. I'm sorry for the betrayal and the abandonment. I'm sorry you weren't supported and cared for. Please know, that is not the heart of God. You have never been forgotten by him, and he has never turned his back on you.

Job experienced it, too. In his trauma, in his hurting, he was met with those same rehearsed answers. He was blamed for his situation. He was told to hurry up and repent. He was ridiculed for his questions and criticized for his angry words. Until God showed up. God came to the ash heap. God appeared in the midst of Job's anger and loss. He didn't wait for Job to have it all figured out. He didn't wait for Job to get his life put back together, and he certainly didn't wait for Job to be healed and back at work tending his sheep and caring for his household before he got involved. Job was in pain. He was hurt, confused, and angry, and God met him there. God meets us in our ashes. He meets us in our pain. As his church we need to do the same. We are called to minister to the broken and the hurting. We are called to share the life and hope found in Jesus. It's time for church leaders and believers to stop offering prettily packaged responses from a safe distance. It's time for us to sit in the ashes with the hurting, our Sunday clothes covered in dirt and grime, our faces lined with tears. Trauma brings people to the ash heap, so that is where the church needs to go.

As the world becomes more aware of mental health and the reality of trauma, the local church needs to be prepared to receive and minister to those who are suffering. And we need to do it in a way that not only honors God but honors the experience of trauma as well. It is my hope that as we journey through the book of Job with an awareness of and sensitivity to the impact of trauma on the biblical text, we will become better equipped to sit with those who are hurting, with the people God has entrusted to our care. The book of Job is a challenging text that raises some of the most difficult questions in the Bible, but it is in the difficulty that we learn, and Job has much to teach us.

A word of transparency at the beginning. . . . I am writing this book from the perspective of a biblical scholar and as someone who has gone through deep wounding. I wrote my dissertation on using trauma theory to interpret the book of Job, and to do that I spent eighteen months of my life researching trauma, trauma therapy, and trauma responses. In the course of that research, I began to see how much the church needs to understand the impact trauma has on survivors and why it is different from other types of sorrow and suffering. I saw in Job's friends people who had been my friends. I saw in Job's agony, my agony. The church is often the place broken and struggling people turn to for help, so we need to be prepared to come alongside them and sit with them in the ashes of their experience. In this book, I will offer what I have learned about trauma and how I see it in the Bible, primarily in the book of Job. I'm simply a Bible scholar who probably reads too much and has a deep desire to serve the church. So, with that disclaimer in mind, I encourage you reach out for professional care if you need it. Trauma is not your fault, it is not a failure, and it is not a sign of weakness. Please do not hesitate to contact a professional mental health care provider if you have experienced trauma, or if you know someone who needs the support and guidance of a licensed therapist.

This book will offer a reading of the book of Job that is informed by an understanding of trauma theory and the impact of trauma. Such a reading is particularly important in today's world, and the lessons we can learn from Job's experience of trauma have immediate applicability in our churches, schools, and families. This book is based on my dissertation "Shattered Theology: A Trauma Theory Reading of the Book of Job," and I have attempted to make it more accessible and immediately applicable (and also shorter and less boring). Trauma theory provides great insight, in my very biased opinion, into the book of Job, but it has its limitations. It cannot and will not answer every question we have about the book of Job. While this book will cover the book of Job from beginning to end, there are several sections of the text and theological questions the text raises that I do not have space to explore. The book of Job is simply too big, and this book would become far too long (and the boring factor would rise exponentially). My narrow focus here is on what the book of Job can teach us about trauma. I do hope you read the book of Job and wrestle with those big questions on your own. There are several excellent commentaries and monographs on the book of Job that can help you, and I joyfully refer you to those talented scholars.[2]

As we begin our journey, chapter one will provide a brief introduction to trauma and trauma responses and the importance of a survivor being able to create a trauma narrative, which is the story they will tell about their experience. Chapter two will then discuss Job's experience of trauma as it is described in the biblical text and his initial responses. Chapter three will look at Job's friends and their reactions to his trauma and how this resonates with many of the typical responses offered by Christian leaders and believers. Chapter

---

[2]While certainly not an exhaustive list, interested readers can start here: Francis I. Anderson, *Job: An Introduction and Commentary* (Downers Grove, IL: InterVarsity Press, 2008); Samuel Balentine, *Job* (Macon, GA: Smyth & Helwys, 2006); David J. A. Clines, *Job 1–20; Job 21–37; Job 38–42* (Grand Rapids, MI: HarperCollins Christian, 1989, 2006, 2015); Gustavo Gutiérrez, *On Job: God-Talk and the Suffering of the Innocent* (Maryknoll, NY: Orbis, 1996); John E. Hartley, *The Book of Job* (Grand Rapids, MI: Eerdmans, 1988); Tremper Longman, *Job*, Baker Commentary on the Old Testament Wisdom and Psalms (Grand Rapids, MI: Baker Academic, 2012); Carol A. Newsom, *The Book of Job: A Contest of Moral Imaginations* (New York: Oxford University Press, 2003); Kathleen O'Connor, *Job* (Collegeville, MN: Liturgical Press, 2012); Eric Ortlund, *Piercing Leviathan: God's Defeat of Evil in the Book of Job* (Downers Grove, IL: InterVarsity Press, 2021); Choon-Leong Seow, *Job 1–21: Interpretation and Commentary* (Grand Rapids, MI: Eerdmans, 2013); John H. Walton, *Job: The NIV Application Commentary* (Grand Rapids, MI: Zondervan, 2012).

four will look at the role of dialogue in the book of Job and what this tells us about the necessity of structure in a trauma narrative to bring some sense of order to the chaos of a traumatic event. Chapter five will focus on the way trauma impacts our language and how we communicate our experience of a traumatic event (spoiler . . . it's usually not well). Chapter six will discuss the importance of justice in trauma resolution. Chapters seven and eight will look at the divine speeches and how they lead to Job's healing as well as Job's restoration in the epilogue and what this teaches us about trauma resolution. Chapter nine will look at the epilogue and what happens to Job after the trauma. Finally, chapter ten will tie all of these threads together in a practical discussion of how we can apply these lessons from the book of Job in our churches, families, and relationships. Each chapter will conclude with some practical takeaways and reflection questions you can think through or use in a small group discussion.

Reading the book of Job through the lens of trauma theory highlights general characteristics of trauma and trauma responses as well as certain elements survivors need to heal from trauma. While such a reading does not answer all of the interpretive difficulties inherent in the book of Job (it's a whopper of a text), it does generate new avenues of conversation and offers the potential to read the biblical text from a perspective that resonates with the life, and struggles, of modern readers. It is also important to acknowledge at the start that the author of the book of Job did not have access to trauma theory vocabulary or research. This is an incontrovertible challenge to using a modern theory to address an ancient text. However, as Brad Kelle points out in his work on moral injury in the biblical texts, "Although the label is recent, the experience it represents is ancient."[3] The need to process traumatic events in order to integrate the experience into a coherent life story may be a modern psychological phrasing, but it

---

[3]Brad E. Kelle, "Moral Injury and Biblical Studies: An Early Sampling of Research and Emerging Trends," *Currents in Biblical Research* 19, no. 2 (February 2021): 124.

is not a modern invention. While the language may be new, the experience of suffering and the need to heal from that suffering is as old as humanity. The author of the book of Job may not have known the words *trauma theory*, but they certainly knew about trauma.

It is my sincere hope that this book will be a resource for trauma survivors as they seek to understand their experiences and heal, and also for church leaders, believers, friends, and family members as they learn how to recognize trauma responses and how to respond in a healthy and caring way. There is no better place for the church to learn than the Bible. The book of Job stands as an incredible testimony to one man's unimaginable experience of trauma and his ultimate healing. However, it also testifies to the many ways we, as leaders and listeners, can fail those who are suffering. Job's friends had an opportunity to be trusted listeners and supporters, but they were so focused on their own agenda and their own theology, that instead they became "miserable comforters" (Job 16:2). In the end, they were rebuked by God. For those of us who long to hear the words "well done my good and faithful servant," as we stand before our King, such a stinging rebuke should challenge us to avoid repeating the mistakes of Job's friends. May we, as God's Church, be those who provide comfort in the ashes.

LESSONS LEARNED

- The book of Job has much to teach survivors and comforters about trauma.
- While a trauma reading approach cannot answer all of the questions about the book of Job, it does have much to offer survivors and the church for recognizing, understanding, and responding to trauma.
- The author of the book of Job was not familiar with modern trauma theory, but the experience of trauma was well-known in the ancient world.

REFLECTION QUESTIONS

- What do you think about the story of Job? Do you have any ideas already about what the text teaches us?

- What is your understanding of trauma? Do you have personal experience with trauma, or have you seen it in others?

- What do you hope to gain from this book?

ONE

WHAT IS TRAUMA?

BEING HUMAN IS AN EXPERIENCE. Our beliefs, worldviews, and approaches to life are often shaped by what we have gone through. Good and bad experiences both leave their mark on us and impact how we view ourselves, others, and the world around us. For example, when I was about five years old, I watched my cousin drink a glass of milk and then immediately throw up. That made such an impression on me, I haven't had a sip of milk since that day. Even though I intellectually know that milk will not make me sick, and even though I bake with milk all the time, I cannot bring myself to drink milk. An experience made a lasting impact on my life and altered how I walk in the world. The circumstances we walk through, the tragedies and joys that fill our lives will have an impact on what we believe and how we live. Our experiences shape our beliefs both for good and for ill. Experience is where the rubber meets the road and our beliefs are formed, tested, and challenged.

Given the connection between experiences and beliefs, it seems not only appropriate but necessary to look at Job's experience of trauma as having a massive impact on his worldview and his fundamental beliefs. Job's losses, his pain, and his response are not a tangential part of the story; they are central to the story. Without the traumatic events he experiences, there is no text. It is the sudden infliction of these traumatic events that sets the book in motion and leads Job, and his friends, through the winding path of theological reflection that ultimately culminates with God showing up in a whirlwind for a chat with Job. In this theological reflection, questions about the nature of God, humanity, retribution, suffering, and redemption appear on almost every page. With such a banquet of deep questions laid before readers, it can be startlingly easy to skip over the personal and intimate details of Job's experience to focus on those big theological issues. Doctrinal debates can easily become more important than people. Sadly, we can see this play out every day on social media. Frenzied replies and name calling dehumanize the person on the other end of the post as debaters and haters focus on proving their point at any cost. We become so determined to defend our theology that we forget to defend God's people.

Now, before we saddle up and ride into a biblical studies debate, let me say that I am not discounting questions of the historicity of Job. Was Job a real person? Is this a factual account of his experience? Or was Job a literary figure made up by the author? Those are interesting issues and they are worth exploring . . . just not here. What we have in front of us is a biblical text that deals with a man named Job and shares his story of terrible affliction and loss. Could it be historical fact? Yes. Could it be a fictional account? Yes. Could it be combination of a real, historical person and a literary creation? Yes. Ultimately, what we are dealing with is Scripture and the primary question is what can we learn from it. In the case of the book of Job we are dealing with Scripture that tells a story of loss, tragedy, suffering, and restoration that is rooted in the depiction of Job's experience.

From beginning to end, it is Job's experience that inspires, guides, and leads the text. It is not enough for us to simply acknowledge that Job suffered and then jump immediately to the abstract theological implications of the text. "Ah yes, Job suffered terribly. Poor chap. Now, let's focus on the big question of where evil comes from, shall we?" Those questions are not wrong, but we must remember that it is Job's experience that challenges his theology. So, to understand his theology, we must understand his experience. This is true in churches today as well. We need to know where someone is walking before we give them advice about their footwear.

This connection between experience and belief is also at the heart of much of our own theological reflection. When bad things happen, when we experience tragedy, loss, or illness, we are often propelled into deep questioning of everything we thought we knew. Our faith in humanity may be shaken, our faith in God may be shaken. Those overwhelming experiences of trauma have an impact on what we believe. We have no choice but to reevaluate the fundamental assumptions we built our lives on. It is important as church leaders and believers that we be aware of this response to trauma so we can meet survivors where they are and walk with them to the other side.

DEFINING TRAUMA

Trauma is a response. Sometimes we see something catastrophic happen or we hear a terrible story and think "that is traumatic." However, when we talk about trauma, what we are really talking about is the response someone has to a terrible event. The event itself is not the trauma. Trauma is the response the survivor has to the event.[1] For example, two people may experience the same catastrophic event, maybe a natural disaster, war, or a car accident, but they may not have the same response. One person may walk away from the event without trauma while the other may experience a trauma response. Both responses are valid and neither implies strength or weakness, great faith or a lack of faith, maturity or immaturity. We are all unique individuals, and we all react to our circumstances differently. Trauma is one possible response to an event.

---

[1]MaryCatherine McDonald, *Unbroken: The Trauma Response Is Never Wrong* (Boulder, CO: Sounds True, 2023), 7.

This is an important distinction because if we, as survivors or comforters, focus on the details of the event, we may find ourselves judging just how traumatic the event was and whether the survivor's response is justified. What may strike us as not such a big deal may, in fact, be a very big deal to the survivor who experiences a trauma response in the aftermath. When we focus on the event instead of the response, we run the risk of introducing shame, blame, and dismissal. Shame conveys to a survivor that their reaction to the event is not appropriate. Blame puts the responsibility for the event on the survivor and thus communicates that they deserve what happened. Dismissal ignores, critiques, or downplays the survivor's response and says, essentially, "get over it." In order to come alongside a survivor in a healthy and compassionate way, we must be willing to let go of our perception of the event and focus on the survivor's response.

The trauma response is an intricate and involuntary network of physical and chemical reactions in the brain and body that take place in response to a threatening event. Please note that I said involuntary. We do not choose to have a trauma response. It is a deeply rooted survival instinct that exists to keep us alive. When we face a threatening situation, we don't have time to analyze all the details, make a list of pros and cons, and form a committee before making a decision. That event may be physical, emotional, spiritual, or something else, but it is an event that triggers a survival response in the brain. If the crocodile is racing toward us, our brain will trigger a survival response without waiting for us to make the conscious decision to run. Ordinarily, the survival response does its job, gets us out of the threatening situation and then resets. But when the survival response lingers and cannot be resolved, when it keeps firing even after the situation has passed, when it shakes the foundations of our world, and we continue to feel unsafe or threatened, that is trauma.[2]

---

[2]Stephen W. Porges and Seth Porges, *Our Polyvagal World: How Safety and Trauma Change Us* (New York: W. W. Norton, 2023).

Now, having said all that, defining trauma is actually not as simple as it sounds. For example, my daughter is a paramedic, and when she says "trauma" she means broken bones, physical injury, and driving fast with lights and sirens blaring. On the other hand, clinical mental health providers who are diagnosing patients for treatment and insurance purposes may rely on a very different definition of trauma found in the current edition of the *Diagnostic and Statistical Manual of Mental Disorders-5-TR* (*DSM-5-TR*). The difficulty here is that this clinical definition of trauma has undergone a series of changes through the years. In its current iteration, the definition of what constitutes trauma is very narrow. John Briere and Catherine Scott, in their textbook on trauma therapy, suggest this current definition unnecessarily excludes many experiences of trauma and therefore underestimates the true prevalence of trauma.[3]

This book you are holding in your hands is not a mental health manual and it is not intended to be used for diagnosis. It is intended to help equip churches to support and minister to trauma survivors and to help survivors heal, so I am choosing to use a broader definition of trauma, one that is still supported by research. The American Psychological Association offers this definition of trauma that will serve as a working definition for us moving forward:

> Any disturbing experience that results in significant fear, helplessness, dissociation, confusion, or other disruptive feelings intense enough to have a long-lasting negative effect on a person's attitudes, behavior, and other aspects of functioning. Traumatic events include those caused by human behavior (e.g., rape, war, industrial accidents) as well as by nature (e.g., earthquakes) and often challenge an individual's view of the world as a just, safe, and predictable place.[4]

---

[3]John Briere and Catherine Scott, *Principles of Trauma Therapy: A Guide to Symptoms, Evaluation, and Treatment* (Thousand Oaks, CA: Sage Publications, 2015), 10.

[4]"Trauma," *APA Dictionary of Psychology*, American Psychological Association, https://dictionary.apa.org/trauma.

This is not meant to discount the importance of the *DSM-5-TR* definition, just as I do not discount my daughter's definition of trauma; it is simply an acknowledgment of two different purposes. So, with that caveat in mind, let's forge ahead.

Trauma is a shattering.[5] Imagine each one of us as having a unique window through which we see the world. We all have certain assumptions, beliefs, and worldviews that color the window we are looking through. Like looking through a stained-glass window that makes trees look blue or landscapes look pink, the colors influence what we see and how we understand it. Those beliefs and assumptions that make up our window affect how we interpret information, how we understand different experiences, and how we process information. It's like our very own mental Instagram filter that is automatically applied to everything. For example, I believe in God. That belief impacts and shapes how I interpret the world around me. If I see a mountain or a platypus or a sunset, I will recognize the incredible creativity and artistry of the God who created those incredible things. However, if I did not believe in a Creator, I might see the mountain, platypus, and sunset, and perhaps think about the amazing accident of nature that brought all those molecules together at just the right time and in just the right way. My belief in God shapes how I interpret those experiences. It is part of the window through which I look at the world. Trauma shatters that window. Trauma shakes and breaks the fundamental beliefs that make up our worldview window. When it falls apart, we lose our window. We no longer have those basic assumptions that helped us interpret and understand the world around us.

Here's another way to think of it: my daughter has terrible eyesight. Terrible. Without glasses or contacts, she can't see anything but different shades of light. She was five years old when we first figured out her eyesight was bad. When we left the optometrist's office with her new glasses,

---

[5]Lisa M. Cataldo, "I Know That My Redeemer Lives: Relational Perspectives on Trauma, Dissociation, and Faith," *Pastoral Psychology* 62, no. 6 (December 2013): 791.

she stopped on the sidewalk and gasped. She pointed to the trees across the parking lot and said, "Those are leaves! There are leaves on the trees!" Her entire life she hadn't seen clearly. Suddenly, with these new glasses, she could see the world. Our worldview, our fundamental beliefs are like those glasses. It impacts how we see the world. When trauma comes crashing in, everything shatters, and we can no longer see clearly.

Trauma is what happens when a rock comes flying through the window. It is not the size of the rock that matters, it is the impact. Even a tiny pebble can shatter a window if it hits just right. That is why we cannot judge someone's reaction as justified or not simply by the event that precipitated it. Pebbles, boulders, river rocks, they can all do unspeakable damage. The way a trauma survivor had previously understood the world is shattered and undone by the rock of the traumatic event. Suddenly everything that seemed certain is questionable. The psychological approach of schema theory presents one way of understanding the impact of this shattering on trauma survivors.[6] A schema is like a file folder in our brain that is stored in our memory. It has a label: *dog*, *pain*, or *love*, and that folder contains our accumulated information about that topic. Basically, these schemas are a way for our minds to process data. Our brains like patterns and pattern recognition, so when we have an experience or encounter new information, our brains want to put it with other similar experiences. Stub my toe? That goes in the minor pain category. Lost my job? That goes in the stress and disappointment (and maybe anger) categories. These schemas help us recognize which experiences are expected, which ones are unexpected, and how to interpret each one. When we encounter something new, our brains pull up one of our existing schemas in order to explain

---

[6]A very technical definition of a schema is "an abstracted knowledge structure, stored in memory, that involves a rich network of information about a given stimulus domain." (Ronnie Janoff-Bulman, "Assumptive Worlds and the Stress of Traumatic Events: Applications of the Schema Construct," *Social Cognition* 7, no. 2 [1989]: 115). For a fuller treatment of schema theory see also Ronnie Janoff-Bulman, *Shattered Assumptions: Towards a New Psychology of Trauma* (New York: The Free Press, 1992).

it. If we imagine our worldview window as a stained-glass window, all of our schemas would make up the different colored panes that fit together to make up the total beautiful mosaic. These schemas make up an entire conceptual system, a window, for processing life experiences.[7] But a trauma-inducing event doesn't fit into any of those schemas. Traumatic events are so far outside the realm of our existing schemas that they threaten to bring down the entire framework.[8] It's like a system overload that makes a machine start smoking and shut down.

Using the psychological framework of schema theory, trauma expert Judith Herman suggests that trauma shatters these inner schemas by which people process and understand the world around them.[9] Trauma is so catastrophic, so outside of the norm, that the inner schemas a person has previously relied on are no longer able to explain the experience. There is, essentially, no way for their mind to fully understand the trauma. Switching up the metaphor for a moment, if we imagine our cognitive framework as a filing cabinet and all of our inner schemas as the files where we categorize and store our experiences, a traumatic experience has no file. It is so far from what we are accustomed to it has no place to go, we have no existing file for it. So, our brain leaves it open, like an item on a to-do list that we can't cross off. The trauma sits in the inbox of our brain, waiting for a place to go, unable to be filed and unable to be ignored. For me, when I have an item on my desk that needs to be completed but I don't know how to do it yet, or I'm missing some piece of information, it sits there on my desk and nags me. I can always see it out of the corner of my eye. I may be working on something else, something totally unrelated, but I know it's there. Waiting. It's like an itch we can't scratch, and so it remains ever-present, and ever-painful.

---

[7] Janoff-Bulman, "Assumptive Worlds," 114.
[8] Janoff-Bulman, "Assumptive Worlds," 116.
[9] Judith Herman, *Trauma and Recovery: The Aftermath of Violence—from Domestic Abuse to Political Terror* (New York: Basic Books), 41.

Theologian Shelly Rambo picks up on this idea of shattering and fragmentation. She writes, "Trauma is described as an encounter with death. This encounter is not, however, a literal death but a way of describing a radical event or events that shatter all that one knows about the world and all the familiar ways of operating within it."[10] The survivor's fundamental beliefs about the world, her safety in it, his perception of the self, and a sense of meaning and order in the world are all called into question by the rupture caused by the traumatic event. It is the cataclysmic destruction of an existing worldview that leaves a void of unmoored confusion.[11] It is only when the trauma survivor can create a new inner schema that is big enough to integrate the traumatic experience in a coherent manner that the trauma will be resolved.[12] We must, essentially, create a new file so the traumatic memory has a place to go . . . and sometimes we have to rebuild the entire filing cabinet.

The overwhelming nature of trauma and the failure of existing schemas to explain the events is one of the cornerstones for understanding a trauma survivor's response. As survivors, we need to create a whole new file, but that is no simple task, and it can be scary. It isn't easy to face such a big challenge to our worldview, especially if it involves beliefs we have held onto for years and have never had a reason to question before. As human beings, we like our existing schemas, and we don't really want to change them. Even when we are faced with a mountain of evidence that our schemas may be wrong, we generally resist changing them.[13] Change can be scary and changing some of our deeply held beliefs . . . well, that is down-right terrifying. This inherent reluctance to changing our schemas is called cognitive conservatism.[14] It's not unlike when they rearrange your grocery store

---

[10]Shelly Rambo, *Spirit and Trauma: A Theology of Remaining* (Louisville, KY: Westminster John Knox, 2010), 4.

[11]Herman, *Trauma and Recovery*, 51.

[12]Herman, *Trauma and Recovery*, 41.

[13]Marcia Webb, "The Book of Job: A Psychologist Takes a Whirlwind Tour," *Christian Scholar's Review* 44, no. 2 (Winter 2015): 158.

[14]Webb, "The Book of Job," 158.

and you want to pitch a fit in the middle of the cereal aisle . . . or what used to be the cereal aisle . . . because you can't find the Lucky Charms. The evidence cannot be denied, the Lucky Charms have been moved, but we may stand in the middle of the now-unfamiliar aisle and try to make things go back to the way they were. Change is disorienting and it can be difficult, especially when it involves our fundamental beliefs or assumptions.

While the precipitating events that may lead to a trauma response can take many disparate forms—war, sexual assault, terrorism, natural disasters, physical, emotional, or spiritual abuse, injury, adultery, medical diagnosis, financial crisis, job loss, and many other types of experiences—it is the *effect* of the event on the survivor that makes it traumatic. What may be a traumatic experience for one person, may not be traumatic for someone else. Two people can experience the same event but process it completely differently. One person may experience a trauma response while the other does not. That does not imply one is stronger or more mature than the other. We all have our own mental schemas. We each have our own filing cabinet. That is why it is so important that we, as comforters, recognize the inherent dignity and uniqueness of each person we encounter. The shattering and the psychic overwhelm of trauma prevent the event from being filed in a survivor's mental filing cabinet and transform the event into the thorn that remains. It doesn't matter what we, as the comforter, think we would have done or how we think we would have responded. What matters is the wounded and hurting person in front of us and how they have responded.

With ordinary events, we experience them, understand them, and file them away without much thought. The traffic jam on the way to work is generally forgotten by lunch. It doesn't linger because we are familiar with the experience, and we know where it goes. When we can file the event away, we understand what happened and we process the emotions tied to it, the event has meaning or a place in the big story of our life, and we can move on and think about other things.

Not so with a trauma-inducing event. The failure of our existing worldview or inner schemas to explain a trauma-inducing event as it occurs creates a gap between the event itself and our filing of the event in our mental filing cabinet. It becomes a "missed encounter."[15] In this missed encounter gap, the event sits in the to-do list pile, and we keep going back to it. Rambo calls this gap between the event and the understanding "the middle."[16] It is in this middle space where the reality of a traumatic event smashes up against a cognitive schema that cannot explain it and results in a crisis of meaning.[17] It is when the rock hits the window, when the event collides with our beliefs, when what we experience crashes into what we know and everything shatters.

In this middle area, trauma makes us ask questions. Big questions. The very nature of the conflict between a lived experience and an established mental schema that cannot explain it leads to a search for another explanation. In other words, the rock broke my window so now I need a new window . . . one that is rock proof. Biblical scholar Christopher Frechette writes, "Traumatic events prompt interpretation, processes by which survivors consciously and unconsciously appropriate what the events mean for them, leading to changes in beliefs about self, others, world and possibly God."[18] Trauma changes us. It forces us to rethink what we thought we knew. The experience doesn't fit anywhere, we don't understand it, we don't get it, and our minds and our bodies react. The traumatic event remains an unresolved and unhealed wound until we can find a way to understand what happened and how it fits into our life. In other words, we will keep stepping on the broken glass and continue to be in pain until we are able to rebuild the window.

---

[15]David G, Garber Jr., "'I Went in Bitterness': Theological Implications of a Trauma Theory in the Reading of Ezekiel," *Review & Expositor* 111, no. 4 (December 2014): 348.

[16]Rambo, *Spirit and Trauma*, 7.

[17]Webb, "The Book of Job," 159.

[18]Christopher G. Frechette, "The Old Testament as Controlled Substance: How Insights from Trauma Studies Reveal Healing Capacities in Potentially Harmful Texts," *Interpretation* 69, no. 1 (January 2015): 25.

Recognizing Trauma

This chapter, while fairly heavy on theory to this point (are you still with me?) gives us an idea of some of the things we can be on the lookout for when it comes to recognizing trauma in the church. Now, this does not necessarily mean trauma *inflicted* in the church or by church leaders. Do churches and pastors inflict trauma? Unfortunately, yes, some do. It's an awful reality that breaks the heart of God and has no place in his kingdom. But sometimes the trauma we will encounter as pastors, church leaders, and believers, will be in people who come to our churches because they are already hurting, because they have been deeply wounded, because they are searching for hope, for help, and for answers. Being able to recognize the possibility of trauma or a trauma response becomes important as we prayerfully consider how to come alongside the suffering. Most churches do not have licensed counseling professionals on staff, and there will be times when the trauma and wounding you encounter will require the intervention of a qualified and licensed professional. Please do not hesitate to refer people to mental health professionals. That is not a failure by you or your church. In fact, it demonstrates wisdom and maturity to recognize when a person needs more help than you or your staff can provide. There is still a place for the church to support someone in their healing who is also working with a professional counselor or doctor. Survivors need community and a healthy local church can provide that community, friendship, and relationship as the survivor heals with the help of a professional. One does not replace the other. As the church we can support, encourage, and walk alongside a survivor and provide them with a community that will love and accept them as they heal.

There will be many times when the church community and leaders can responsibly and ethically minister to someone who is a trauma survivor. Understanding what makes trauma so fundamentally different from other types of sorrow, sadness, depression, anger, or disorientation is vital to being a help and not a hinderance in their healing journey. The church is meant to be a safe place where the broken can find healing and the suffering can find solace. Unfortunately, we have often turned it into a business or a brand, a self-perpetuating institution running on getting people in the pews and money in the buckets. But Jesus told us that *we* are the church. Not a building or a platform, people are the body of Christ and when one person hurts, we, as the church, hurt too. From the pastor to the newest believer, we are all broken and in need of healing in some way; trauma is just one aspect of the beautifully broken and wonderfully healing body of Christ.

So how can we recognize trauma? The above discussion, though brief, highlights some of the defining characteristics. It is overwhelming, unable to be immediately processed, and challenges our fundamental assumptions about the world. We may see this overwhelming nature when a trauma survivor has difficulty remembering the event. Because traumatic events and trauma memories are "missed" they are not processed neatly and logically like ordinary memories, so the survivor's memory of the experience may be jumbled and fragmented. Instead of reacting with suspicion—Did that really happen? Why is your story changing? Are you sure about that?—recognize that traumatic memories are messy, disconnected, and chaotic. This is to be expected, and it is a normal part of a trauma response. You wouldn't walk into a room with a broken window and expect all the pieces to be organized by size and color on the floor, right? When a window shatters, we will find broken pieces scattered everywhere—under a chair, on top of a picture frame, on a shelf—and it will take several inspections to make sure we picked up all the pieces, and even then, we may find ourselves stepping on a stray shard of glass in our bare feet months later. Understand that the survivor's memories of a traumatic event exist in a different form and in a different cognitive space. Be patient as they try to reassemble them.

Next, as trauma survivors we may have difficulty talking about the trauma. This goes beyond a simple reluctance to talk about something bad. I have a few middle school memories I don't want to talk about, not because they are traumatic but because it was the 1980s and I was given unfettered access to blue eyeliner and aerosol hair spray. It's not that I can't talk about those days, I am choosing not to talk about them (and burying the photos in a box in the garage that no one will ever open). Trauma, on the other hand, has a physiological impact on the brain that can make expressing or talking about the event difficult. Trauma theorists expect this crisis of language in the wake of a traumatic experience. As Webb explains, "trauma—as cognitive material which cannot immediately be integrated into broader schematic representations of reality—may be accompanied by sudden language deficits."[19] This is not a statement about the intelligence of the survivor, rather it is an acknowledgment of the impact of trauma on language itself. It is not simply an issue of a trauma survivor not wanting to talk about their experience, though that may also be present, but it is an issue of the physiological effect trauma has on our ability to speak about it.[20]

Bessel van der Kolk's neuroscientific research on trauma has demonstrated this physiological impact of trauma. He has noted a lowered function in Broca's area in the brain which is one of our primary speech centers.[21] He writes, "Without a functioning Broca's area, you cannot put your thoughts and feelings into words."[22] Trauma hits this speech center of the brain and pauses it, so it doesn't function the way it normally does. Trauma, as a survival response, shuffles energy

---

[19]Webb, "The Book of Job," 162.
[20]Kathleen O'Connor, *Lamentations and the Tears of the World* (Maryknoll, NY: Orbis Books, 2015), 5.
[21]Bessel van der Kolk, *The Body Keeps the Score: Brain, Mind, and Body in the Healing of Trauma* (New York: Penguin, 2014), 43. For an additional discussion on the physiological impact of trauma, see also Dr. Stephen Porges's work on polyvagal theory and the role of the vagus nerve in trauma responses.
[22]van der Kolk, *The Body Keeps the Score*, 43.

around to prioritize survival. The job of the survival response is to keep the victim alive, to get them through the ordeal, so the brain and body work together to prioritize the things the person needs to survive. Things like the speech center and memory storage are less of a priority when the issue is survival. When we are running from the crocodile, we don't need to talk more, we need to run faster, so the brain puts more energy into our running than it does to our talking. This combination of psychological and physiological effects of trauma has a significant impact on the survivor's ability to express themselves and describe their experience. There are literally no words. Imagine living in the first century and by some strange feat of time travel or space portals, you see an airplane. You are the only person who saw it. It was there and then gone. How would you describe it to your community? None of your normal words or adjectives would work. You've never seen anything like it before and neither has anyone else. You don't know what it was, and you have no idea how to describe it. Trauma is like that. There simply are no words.

We must also recognize the crisis of meaning prompted by trauma. When the window shatters, the survivor cannot simply order a new window and patiently sip their tea while they wait for their two-day delivery truck to arrive. The pieces have to be picked up, and this process is messy. There are sharp edges everywhere. Many survivors will engage in repetitious behavior while trying to heal from trauma. This may be simply repeating a story about the trauma or talking about the same thing over and over. What others may perceive as "not letting it go," or "obsessing over it," may, in fact, be an important step in their healing process. Like that to-do list item in our inbox, we have to keep going back to it until we know how to tackle it. Repetition may also be physical repetition as the survivor returns to the scene of the trauma or continues similar behavior patterns. It may be present in flashbacks, nightmares, or intrusive thoughts that appear without warning as the mind returns again and again to the event. Repetition, in its many forms, is an expected trauma response. Because the mind doesn't know how to categorize the event or how to file it away, it has to return to it over and over attempting each time to figure out what it is and where it fits. But trauma does not fit easily. Perhaps it's a bit like working on a jigsaw puzzle and you keep picking up that one odd-shaped piece because you know it has to fit somewhere, but you haven't found the place yet. As comforters, it can be exhausting and even frustrating to hear someone say the same thing over and over again, or if they seem to reject our well-intentioned advice. We may try to push them to move on, to get over it, but the repetition that seems unnecessary to us may, in fact, be a vital part of their healing process. Survivors may need to pick up that piece over and over until they figure out where it goes. As comforters, it is not our job to rush the process, but to support survivors as they work through it. However, as important as repetition can be, we definitely don't want anyone to return to an abusive or dangerous situation, and that may be a time to involve professionals or law enforcement.

Finally, trauma messes with a survivor's nervous system. The presence of observable physiological changes in survivors illustrates that trauma is not simply in our mind, it's also in our body. A trauma response can include a physical reaction to an overwhelming experience. Trauma can effectively rewire a survivor's nervous system. The autonomic nervous system that functions to help us survive in life-threatening situations can be impacted by trauma. Dr. Stephen Porges suggests that the vagus nerve responds to how safe we feel.[23] When we feel unsafe (notice that says when we *feel* unsafe, not necessarily that we *are* unsafe) our fight/flight/freeze survival instinct can switch on involuntarily as our body instinctually acts to keep us alive.[24] The challenge arises when we get stuck in this survival mode or when we are triggered into it by something that isn't a genuine threat. We often

---

[23]Porges, *Our Polyvagal World*, 27.
[24]Porges, *Our Polyvagal World*, 28.

see this manifesting in survivors in panic attacks, anxiety, hypervigilance, distrust, and physical symptoms like stomach distress, illness, migraines, and the list goes on. The complexity of a survivor's nervous system and the way it is intertwined with memories, even just fragmented and disorderly snippets, of the traumatic event may lead to a reaction that is beyond the survivor's control. Panic attacks, freezing, anger: a survivor can have a wide range of responses to a triggering event. Our nervous system reacts without our consent and without our planning. It is an immediate reaction to what is perceived as a threatening situation. Remember, our minds and our bodies like patterns. Trauma stitches together certain memories of the traumatic event with our survival instinct to protect us from further harm. When that alarm gets triggered, even if it's a false alarm, the nervous system is off and running. For trauma survivors this can be incredibly disorienting. We may feel like we are hopelessly lost with no way out. We may feel like things will never change. We may feel like there is something wrong with us. What we need to remember is that a trauma response does not mean we're broken; it is simply a sign that our survival instinct needs help to reset.

When our military family moved across the country (again) we rented a house on a golf course for a few months. At one point a golf ball flew way off course and smashed into one of the windows. The window didn't break, but it was hopelessly cracked. Our landlord sent a window repair company out to replace it. When that golf ball smashed into the window we didn't move out. Our landlord didn't throw up his hands and sell the house because it was broken and useless now. It was just a window that needed to be repaired. Just as trauma shatters a survivor's window and may trigger an involuntary response, the survivor is not broken. It is just one part of them that needs to be recognized, honored, and helped. A trauma response is not a sign of weakness or immaturity or a lack of faith. A trauma response is part of how God designed us. A trauma response protects us from harm and helps us survive situations no human being should have to go through. That is a miraculous and beautiful thing. We would do well to recognize the good that response did in the moment, and then focus on how we can honor the trauma and help the survivor resolve it.

To the outside witness, these reactions may not make sense. As comforters, we may not understand how a leadership meeting at church triggers a new member to have a panic attack. What is quite simple and enjoyable for us is setting off all kinds of alarms in the survivor's nervous system. Maybe it is a word or a phrase that brings up a memory of betrayal and that connection between the memory and the trauma causes a trigger and panic ensues. Maybe it is a smell that triggers a connection to a car accident, or a whiff of cologne that takes a survivor back to a sexual assault. Maybe it is a television show or a sound that takes the survivor's mind back to the loss of a loved one. The connections the mind makes between these fragmentary memories and the initial trauma is a type of pattern recognition. The mind wants to categorize things and recognize patterns so it knows how to respond. When this happens with a traumatic event, the mind digs up the original survival response and instinctively returns to it to protect the survivor from further harm. What seems like an overreaction or an out-of-the-blue response to us as witnesses is actually a complex and involuntary response by the survivor's nervous system. We must remember that we did not go through their trauma—they did. It is their nervous system that is reacting in a way that is meant to protect and defend against further wounding. What doesn't make sense to us makes perfect sense to the survivor's nervous system. As leaders and believers who are in positions to minister to trauma survivors, recognizing the complexity of this connection between a traumatic event and physical reactions is important, and it will require us to be willing to accept what we don't understand. No, a pastor saying the word *family* shouldn't send someone into a panic attack, but it did. That is an opportunity for us to meet a survivor in the ashes of their trauma, sit with them, and learn about their experience without imposing our assessment of the situation on them. To reply with something like "that's not what I meant, you're overreacting" is not helpful. It may have been a completely safe and even loving situation, but the survivor's nervous system did exactly what it is meant to do . . . it recognized potential danger and sent up a warning flare. The difficulty with trauma is that it can associate danger in the wrong places. That will take time to rewire and heal.

To sit with someone in their trauma and in their pain should be a ministry of presence, not pressure. They may need to talk about what happened to them a dozen times, a hundred times. Each time is serving a purpose. It is our privilege as the church to provide a safe space for that processing. We will explore more characteristics of trauma and trauma responses throughout the following chapters as we look at Job and his experience, but for now, two important points remain. First, recognizing our limitations as comforters and knowing when to refer someone to professional care is responsible, wise, and ethical. Second, as Christian leaders and believers it is not our job to sweep away someone's ashes and drag them to their feet. It is our task to meet them in the midst of the grime and be present.

The Three Stages of Trauma Recovery

In order to get to a place of trauma resolution, a place where the outstanding file finds a home in our mental filing cabinet and the shattered window is rebuilt, a trauma survivor must first engage in the work of "adaptive rumination."[25] Adaptive rumination is a scholarly way of saying that we are willing to do the hard work of rethinking our schemas and rebuilding our window. This process is the opposite of cognitive conservatism, or the resistance to changes in our worldview. It allows for the possibility of letting go of long-held schemas in

---

[25]Webb, "The Book of Job," 161.

favor of rebuilding a more comprehensive framework that can enfold the totality of the survivor's experiences. For example, if we are convinced that good things happen to good people and bad things happen only to bad people, what will we do if we are struck with a sudden illness or loss? In the face of our own experience, we may find ourselves needing to rethink that basic assumption. If I've been a good person, why did this bad thing happen to me? That is a shattered schema that needs to be rebuilt, but we cannot build a new schema unless we're ready to let go of the old one, right? In this rebuilding process, the trauma survivor "faces a double task: not only must she rebuild her own 'shattered assumptions' about meaning, order, and justice in the world but she must also find a way to resolve differences with those whose beliefs she can no longer share."[26] Not only do we have to rebuild our own window, but we have to figure out how our new window fits in with the rest of the neighborhood.

Beyond the mental healing and adaptive rumination that is necessary for the trauma to be resolved, Herman suggests three stages of recovery for a trauma: establishing safety, remembrance and mourning, and reconnection with ordinary life.[27] Establishing safety generally refers to immediate physical safety. Is the trauma survivor physically safe? Are they at risk for abuse? Are they in danger? Safety also refers to emotional, mental, and spiritual safety. As Christian leaders, we can work to make sure our churches are safe places for healing where members are protected from abuse and exploitation. Scot McKnight and Laura Barringer highlight this in their outstanding book *A Church Called Tov*.[28] They offer several important elements of a church centered on *tov*, or goodness, including nurturing empathy and grace, putting people first, telling the truth, and

---

[26]Herman, *Trauma and Recovery*, 178.
[27]Herman, *Trauma and Recovery*, 155.
[28]Scot McKnight and Laura Barringer, *A Church Called Tov: Forming a Goodness Culture That Resists Abuses of Power and Promotes Healing* (Carol Stream, IL: Tyndale House, 2020).

nurturing justice, service, and Christlikeness.[29] In order to minister to the wounded we must first cultivate an environment of safety.

A significant portion of the following chapters will focus on the second stage of recovery, remembrance and mourning, because that constitutes much of what we see in the book of Job. The book of Job, in many ways, resembles a trauma narrative. A trauma narrative is an intentionally crafted testimony or retelling of the traumatic event that allows for survivors to begin to integrate it into their mental filing cabinet. Since the traumatic event was cognitively missed when it occurred, the trauma narrative becomes a way to reengage with the missed encounter and process it. There are several important similarities between the book of Job and trauma narratives that offer interpretive insights that not only help us understand the text, but they also help us understand how trauma survivors process their experiences and how we, as trusted listeners and comforters in a local church body, can support that journey.

Because a traumatic event is not processed and filed as it occurs, the trauma becomes disconnected from the rest of the survivor's life story and memories. It's like a puzzle piece that doesn't fit. Even better, it's like a puzzle piece from an entirely different puzzle. We don't know what to do with it. Traumatic memories often exist not as a cohesive story with a beginning, middle, and end, but as fragments and images, snippets of sensory memories, a smell, or a sound, or a fleeting picture that pops into our brains. The traumatic event caused a rupture in our life story. We may even look at our life in two pieces, before the trauma and after the trauma, with the traumatic event itself as the middle turning point. A trauma narrative functions as a way to help give coherence and meaning to the traumatic event and bring it into one, complete story of our life. In a trauma narrative, the events begin to be understood in a way that the mind can recognize, incorporate, and

---

[29]McKnight and Barringer, *A Church Called Tov*, 97.

file. The construction of a trauma narrative can help provide structure, expression, and meaning to an otherwise incomprehensible experience. When this trauma narrative is coupled with adaptive rumination and a new, more resilient cognitive schema, the trauma survivor can begin to experience healing and wholeness. This is not an easy process, and the survivor will need support, compassion, and trusted listeners along the way.

The third stage in trauma recovery is reconnection with the community. In the coming chapters we will look at how Job's friends react to his trauma and what happens to their relationship through the course of the text. The ugly truth is trauma often results in social isolation and loneliness. This can happen for a few reasons. It may be that the overwhelming nature of the trauma and the hypervigilance, distrust, and fear that often results may make social interactions difficult, even terrifying, for a survivor. It may also be that the survivor's community and support system simply don't know how to respond. Often, as human beings, when we don't know what to do we choose to do nothing. We may stay on the sidelines, giving the survivor "space" and waiting until things blow over. Many trauma survivors find themselves alone because their experience is frightening, disorienting, and confusing, not just to them, but to those around them as well. Trauma has ripples and oftentimes those ripples carry much further than we know. A survivor's community is in a unique position to be of great help or great harm. How the survivor's community responds to their experience and the healing process is incredibly important. If handled well, the community can be one of the biggest contributors to a survivor's healing. If handled poorly, the community can be a cause of additional wounding, suffering, and pain.

Be warned, the journey is not a straight line from trauma to healing with boxes to check off and schedules to follow. There are twists and turns and curves and setbacks and for survivors and comforters this can be challenging. There is no map in trauma recovery, and there is no timeline. Trauma survivors have experienced the worst this world has to offer. The storm is raging and it's dark and scary, but there is another side. There is joy on the other side. There is purpose and laughter on the other side. Between Good Friday and Easter Sunday there is the silence of Saturday. That is where the trauma lies, in the middle space, where everything seems lost, and we can't imagine how it will all work out. God calls us to walk with our brothers and sisters as they find their way through the middle and emerge into the light and promise of Sunday.

LESSONS LEARNED

- Trauma is a response to an event. We cannot decide how traumatic something is for someone else. We must be humble and curious as we learn about a survivor's experience.

- Trauma responses have both psychological and physiological characteristics. Trauma is not a sign of weakness, immaturity, or lack of faith. Our survival instinct was designed by God to help keep us alive.

- Healing from trauma is a process that will have ups and downs. Our community can play an important role in healing from trauma.

REFLECTION QUESTIONS

- Are there any times you have judged yourself or others for how they are suffering?

- How does knowing that trauma is not just in the mind but in the body as well impact how you view people who are suffering?

- What does a healthy church for trauma survivors look like?

....

TWO

JOB'S EXPERIENCE OF TRAUMA

SETTING THE SCENE

No one can doubt that Job suffered. In fact, if there was a picture of suffering in the dictionary it might be an image of Job. He loses all of his children in a freak accident, his wealth (measured in those days by livestock) is stolen, his servants are killed, and then he is inflicted with painful sores from the bottom of his feet to the top of his head. He ends up on an ash heap outside of town scraping his oozing sores with pieces of broken pottery. I think that definitely qualifies as suffering. There are several key areas where the book of Job reflects trauma, and that is what we are going to focus on. Understanding trauma helps us study the book of Job and studying the book of Job helps us understand trauma. But before we can dig into how that works, we need to set the scene. How did Job end up on the ash heap?

The text begins with something of a "once upon a time" type opening. We learn of a man named Job who lives in the land of Uz. Where Uz may have been we don't know. What we do know is that Job is a righteous man who is incredibly wealthy and devoted to his family and to God. The text then takes a strange turn, and we suddenly find our-selves in the heavenly realm. Many readers of the book of Job get stuck in this opening section of the text. First, there is a meeting in a heavenly council, which brings up some valid theological questions to begin with, but in the midst of this meeting a figure called *hassatan* shows up. Now, there are readers who suggest this is the same Satan character that we read about in the New Testament, but I disagree.[1] In the Hebrew, the definite article *ha* is attached to the front of the word. This definite article *ha* translates as "the," and *satan* translates as "accuser" or "challenger." *Hassatan* then might be more accurately translated as The Satan, as if it is the title of a position, and not the figure's personal name.[2] What we know of this figure is that it functions as an accuser. Whether this is the Satan figure we have come to associate with the devil or whether this figure is something else entirely, what we do know from the text is that *hassatan* shows up to this council meeting, where it is God himself who points out Job. The text reads,

> The LORD said to the accuser [*hassatan*], "Have you considered my servant Job? There is no one like him on the earth, a blameless and upright man who fears God and turns away from evil." (Job 1:8)

God is drawing attention to Job as a blameless and upright man. He even refers to Job as "my servant," which is high praise indeed. The phrase "my servant" in the Hebrew Bible is used to refer to Abraham, Moses, and David. It is not a passing compliment; it is a significant

---

[1] Clines similarly argues that this figure in the book of Job is not the same as the Satan in New Testament writing and later theology (David J. A. Clines, *Job 1–20* [Grand Rapids, MI: Harper-Collins Christian, 1989], 20). The question of the identity of the *hassatan* figure takes us off the trauma track, so I won't devote much time to it. Several scholars have addressed the issue: Clines, *Job 1–20*; John E. Hartley, *The Book of Job* (Grand Rapids, MI: Eerdmans, 1988); Tremper Longman, *Job*, Baker Commentary on the Old Testament Wisdom and Psalms (Grand Rapids, MI: Baker Academic, 2012); Choon-Leong Seow, *Job 1–21: Interpretation and Commentary* (Grand Rapids, MI: Eerdmans, 2013); and John H. Walton, *Job: The NIV Application Commentary* (Grand Rapids, MI: Zondervan, 2012). I am most persuaded by the argument that the *hassatan* figure functions as an accuser in the heavenly council, something like a prosecuting attorney, rather than the enemy of the church we find described later in the New Testament.
[2] See, for example, Walton, *Job*, 67.

and meaningful designation that is given to Job by God himself. But *hassatan* is unimpressed. In fact, he argues that Job only serves God because God has blessed him in so many ways.

> Then the accuser answered the LORD, "Does Job fear God for nothing? Have you not put a fence around him and his house and all that he has, on every side? You have blessed the work of his hands, and his possessions have increased in the land. But stretch out your hand now, and touch all that he has, and he will curse you to your face." (Job 1:9-11)

In other words, *hassatan* says, "Job doesn't really love you, God. He only loves you because of all the stuff you do for him. Take away those blessings and see what happens." *Hassatan* has essentially reduced Job's relationship with God to a transaction. God blesses Job, so Job praises God. It is a critique, not just of Job, but of the entire system *hassatan* thinks God has set up. John Walton refers to this transactional-type of theology as the "Retribution Principle."[3] If you do good things, God will bring good things to you. If you do bad things, God will punish you with bad things. This concept of retribution will become an important element in the coming chapters as Job and his friends try to explain Job's circumstances.

Then, in an astounding plot twist, instead of arguing the point with *hassatan*, God allows *hassatan* to inflict terrible losses on Job. His oxen, sheep, and camels are stolen, his servants are killed, and his children die when the house they are gathered in collapses. This is a huge point of theological "say what?" Why would God allow his faithful servant to be treated this way? Let's be honest here, this is a difficult passage to read. Why does God allow this to happen? Unfortunately, the book of Job does not give us an easy answer to that question, something we will look at in a later chapter when it comes to understanding our own trauma and suffering. Yet, after all these unexplained disasters, Job does not curse God as *hassatan* expected.

---

[3]Walton, *Job*, 68.

> Then Job arose, tore his robe, shaved his head, and fell on the ground and worshiped. He said, "Naked I came from my mother's womb, and naked shall I return there; the LORD gave, and the LORD has taken away; blessed be the name of the LORD." In all this Job did not sin or charge God with wrongdoing. (Job 1:20-22)

Job has passed the test. Even when he loses everything, he does not curse God. But *hassatan* is not convinced. Instead, he shows up at another council meeting and when God praises Job for his response, *hassatan* suggests pushing Job further.

> The LORD said to the accuser, "Have you considered my servant Job? There is no one like him on the earth, a blameless and upright man who fears God and turns away from evil. He still persists in his integrity, although you incited me against him, to destroy him for no reason." Then the accuser answered the LORD, "Skin for skin! All that the man has he will give for his life. But stretch out your hand now and touch his bone and his flesh, and he will curse you to your face." The LORD said to the accuser, "Very well, he is in your power; only spare his life." (Job 2:3-6)

Now we find Job covered in painful sores and exiled to the ash heap. Trauma after trauma after trauma. The text is very clear: Job has done nothing wrong. He does not deserve what has happened to him. He doesn't understand why it has happened, and yet we're told again, "in all this Job did not sin with his lips" (Job 2:10b). At this point, Job has seemingly passed the second round of testing, and yet, the story does not end there.

It's at this point Job's three friends show up. They have heard about his suffering, and they get together and decide to go and "console and comfort him" (Job 2:11b). Remember those words because they will become important in later chapters as we look at the role of trusted listeners and support systems for trauma survivors. These three friends wanted to console Job in his time of suffering and comfort him. Sounds good, right? When they show up, they don't even recognize Job. Once they realize this dejected and diseased human sitting in the town garbage dump is their friend, they burst into tears. They tear their clothes, throw dust on their heads, and sit with him in the ashes for seven days and no one says a word. After seven days, Job finally speaks, and everything gets messy.

Job's Silence

At the conclusion of this opening section in the book of Job, readers are left with silence. Job has lost nearly everything but his life. His wealth and his resources have been stolen, his reputation is ruined, his children have been killed, and finally his health fails. The second chapter concludes with this passage:

> Now when Job's three friends heard of all these troubles that had come on him, each of them set out from his home—Eliphaz the Temanite, Bildad the Shuhite, and Zophar the Naamathite. They met together to go and console and comfort him. When they saw him from a distance, they did not recognize him, and they raised their voices and wept aloud; they tore their robes and threw dust in the air on their heads. They sat with him on the ground seven days and seven nights, and no one spoke a word to him, for they saw that his suffering was very great. (Job 2:11-13)

The first two chapters of the book of Job are written in prose and the first verse in chapter three will start the long, poetic middle of the book. But between Job 2:13 and Job 3:1 there is silence. The temptation to rush past this subtle transition and dive into Job's speech in Job 3 is great. However, when we're dealing with trauma, silence speaks volumes.

What we have in the text, is, essentially, literary silence. The importance of this silence goes beyond a potential connection with a ritualized mourning period or functioning as a transitionary piece between the prose of the opening and the poetry of the middle section. Elizabeth Boase notes, "In the failing of words and the limits of language, textual silences may be more than gaps in need of filling, more than open spaces that invite readers to read into an indeterminacy of meaning. Silences may, in fact, be expressive of incommunicability itself."[4] The silence in the text is itself a testimony to the depth of Job's trauma. Sometimes bad things are so bad that we can't find the words to describe them. This failure of language is one of the characteristics of trauma. It is also worth noting here that Job is not the only biblical character who is reduced to textual silence in the face of trauma. By textual silence, I mean that the characters are not given a voice in the text. Their words, and therefore their perspective, their interpretation of the events, their wounds and their hurts as well as their healing are not included in the narrator's depiction of the events. For example, Jacob's daughter Dinah is textually silent after she is raped (Gen 34:1-4). Readers have no idea how she felt or what her reaction to the rape looked like. We are only told of what her brothers thought and did. Similarly, Tamar is silent in the aftermath of rape and rejection by Amnon (2 Sam 13). She tries to advocate for herself and is thrown out into the streets and reduced to silence. In the book of Judges, the Levite's concubine who is sacrificed to the mob is never given a voice as she is thrown into the street to face rape and murder (Judg 19:22-26). The textual silence of biblical characters who suffer trauma is noteworthy for its connection with modern understandings of the impact and effects of trauma on survivors. These gaps in the text, these literary silences, are not empty, but instead may testify to the presence of trauma. Most of us have had an experience that is so shocking that we have nothing to say. It is the silence itself that demonstrates the magnitude of the moment. It isn't easy to recognize silence in a text because we just keep reading, but our tendency to rush past these silences may cause us to miss the reality of the human experience contained within the silence.

Job's silence is, therefore, not a lack of response. It is instead a testifying response to trauma. In fact, silence is a common response to a

---

[4]Elizabeth Boase, "'Whispered in the Sound of Silence': Traumatising the Book of Jonah," *The Bible and Critical Theory* 12, no. 1 (2016): 8.

traumatic experience.[5] When words fail, we may rely on nonverbal means of communication.[6] This observation is supported by the text in the book of Job. In the aftermath of a series of traumatic losses, Job resorts to nonverbal expressions of his suffering. Job removes himself from his community and sits in the ashes (Job 2:8b). He scrapes himself with a potsherd (Job 2:8a). Job becomes so disfigured, so physically changed, that his friends do not recognize him at first (Job 2:12). His friends similarly tear their clothes and toss dust on their heads (Job 2:12b). Then they sit on the ground in silence (Job 2:13a). The trauma Job experiences may not be able to be expressed in language in the beginning, but the nonverbal actions in this section testify in the silence.

As church leaders and comforters, we can be attuned to these nonverbal indicators of trauma. Have you noticed someone slumping and looking down? Are they crying? Are they continually at the altar or with the prayer team asking for prayer, even if they can't specify the reason? What are the outside indicators that are different for this person? Has their dress changed? Has their hygiene changed? Were they faithful attenders, but now they are suddenly missing from church services? What signs of stress or sorrow or grief can you observe? Do you know a life-changing event has occurred, but they haven't said anything about it? Or have they seemed to bounce back from a tragedy abnormally quickly? The overwhelming nature of trauma and the time it takes for a survivor to recognize how everything has changed will take time to progress. We cannot assume a survivor's first response will be their final response. Job didn't immediately switch from "blessed be the name of the Lord" to cursing the day of his birth. It took days, perhaps weeks or even longer for him to get to that point. We can't mistake silence for nothingness. Sometimes the silence itself is the cry for help.

---

[5]Bessel van der Kolk, *The Body Keeps the Score: Brain, Mind, and Body in the Healing of Trauma* (New York: Penguin, 2014), 43.
[6]Joseph Cauchi, "Ezekiel 21:1-22 as Trauma Literature," *Australian Biblical Review* 69 (2021): 21.

In fact, Webb argues that this textual representation of silence is an important testimony to trauma. "The biblical characters [in the book of Job] reflect the psychological truth that silence in the presence of trauma is not about nothing; on the contrary, it signifies the magnitude of the situation before them."[7] Remember, one of the hallmarks of trauma is that it cannot be immediately categorized by our minds. We don't have a label for something so far outside of our worldview and schemas. We literally don't have any words to describe trauma, because we don't really know what it is yet. So, silence should not be a surprise. Silence *is* the description because silence is all we have. Silence follows trauma because of the overwhelming nature of the traumatic experience and an accompanying inability to explain the experience. When existing schemas and modes of explanation fail, the survivor may turn to silence. The experience is inexpressible and so silence becomes our only option.

It is this silence that paves the way for Job's speech in Job 3. Without an acknowledgment of the importance of Job's silence, the abrupt transition in the text from prose to poetry, from Job's perceived initial acceptance of his circumstances to his later poetic outrage will confound and confuse us as readers. We may wonder why the switch from prose to poetry occurs. Why there? What happened to make Job suddenly change his tone? What are we missing? Was the text corrupted? Is it the work of different authors? What happened here? But trauma research tells us there is no additional event needed to justify the change in genre or the change in Job's tone and content. The silence itself *is* the explanation.

A Traumatic Rupture

After the silence that ends Job 2, Job begins to speak. The anticipation of his words is fraught with tension as the crux of the discussion in the heavenly council was the issue of Job's words. Job has lost just

---

[7]Webb, "The Book of Job," 163.

about everything and suddenly his silence ends. Will he curse God? Whose estimation of Job will be proven right? The Joban poet writes, "After this Job opened his mouth and cursed the day of his birth" (Job 3:1). So, Job does indeed utter a curse, but it is not against God, at least not directly. Instead, he curses the day of his birth:

> After this Job opened his mouth and cursed the day of his birth. Job said:
>
> "Let the day perish in which I was born,
>> and the night that said,
>>> 'A male is conceived.'
>> Let that day be darkness!
>>> May God above not seek it
>>> or light shine on it.
>> Let gloom and deep darkness claim it.
>>> Let clouds settle upon it;
>>> let the blackness of the day terrify it.
>> That night—let thick darkness seize it!
>>> let it not rejoice among the days of the year;
>>> let it not come into the number of the months.
>> Yes, let that night be barren;
>>> let no joyful cry be heard in it.
>> Let those curse it who curse the Sea,
>>> those who are skilled to rouse up Leviathan.
>> Let the stars of its dawn be dark;
>>> let it hope for light but have none;
>>> may it not see the eyelids of the morning—
>> because it did not shut the doors of my mother's womb
>>> and hide trouble from my eyes.
>
> "Why did I not die at birth,
>> come forth from the womb and expire?
> Why were there knees to receive me
>> or breasts for me to suck?

Now I would be lying down and quiet;
    I would be asleep; then I would be at rest
with kings and counselors of the earth
    who rebuild ruins for themselves,
or with princes who have gold,
    who fill their houses with silver.
Or why was I not buried like a stillborn child,
    like an infant that never sees the light?
There the wicked cease from troubling,
    and there the weary are at rest.
There the prisoners are at ease together;
    they do not hear the voice of the taskmaster.
The small and the great are there,
    and the slaves are free from their masters.

"Why is light given to one in misery
    and life to the bitter in soul,
who long for death, but it does not come,
    and dig for it more than for hidden treasures;
who rejoice exceedingly
    and are glad when they find the grave?
Why is light given to one who cannot see the way,
    whom God has fenced in?
For my sighing comes like my bread,
    and my groanings are poured out like water.
Truly the thing that I fear comes upon me,
    and what I dread befalls me.
I am not at ease, nor am I quiet;
    I have no rest, but trouble comes." (Job 3:1-26)

It is safe to say that Job's tone and perspective has undergone a significant change from "the Lord gave and the Lord has taken away, blessed be the name of the Lord" in Job 1. I'm not exaggerating when I say that through the centuries this chapter has been hotly debated. There is no true consensus on its meaning or even its genre. Is it a death wish? Is it an indirect curse of God? Is it a wish to destroy all of creation? Is it manipulative? Does Job say it even though he knows it would be ineffective because of a *Hot Tub Time Machine* type of paradox . . . if Job got his wish and had never been born, he would not be alive to utter that wish and so it wouldn't be fulfilled and he would, in fact, still be born. It can make your head spin. As with all poetry, the multivalent nature, meaning multiple possible meanings, of the content and the artistry of the form leave much room for interpretation. However, the primary question for us, at the moment, is what does this chapter tell us about trauma and what trauma survivors need?

One of the first things we notice about Job 3 is that it is written in poetry. Go back with me to our first metaphor of trauma: a rock shattering a window. Trauma is a rupture, an interruption, an unexpected and unanticipated intrusion into something that seemed solid, steady, and predictable. Job's life was running along quite smoothly. He was managing his household, praying for his children, and serving God. Then out of nowhere . . . BAM . . . trauma. A rock comes crashing through the window of his life and shatters everything he thought he knew. A trauma-inducing event is that out-of-nowhere, didn't-see-it-coming, never-imagined-this-would-happen-to-me kind of experience. It bursts onto the scene and throws everything into chaos.

What is fascinating about the book of Job (among many things) is how this is represented in the text. The first two chapters of the book of Job are written in prose. Job 2 ends with him and his friends sitting in silence. No one speaks to Job; no one knows what to say. There is literary silence in the text. When Job speaks again in the opening of Job 3, he speaks in poetry. The genre of the text abruptly switches with no explanation or warning. Prose one sentence, poetry next. The prose is interrupted by the poetry, just like Job's life is interrupted by trauma. The poetry will continue until the closing chapter of the book where the prose will resume, again without warning or explanation. One sentence is poetry, then suddenly the next sentence is prose. The book of Job is thus framed by the prose prologue and the prose epilogue. The messy middle is poetry. This prose framing highlights the rupture of trauma. The straightforward, logical narrative of prose is interrupted by the artistic, figurative, nonlinear form of poetry. The prose does not start again until Job is able to resolve his trauma. We'll look at this in more depth in a following chapter, but for now, it's important that we recognize the intrusive and disruptive nature of trauma, and how this is illustrated in the book of Job.

There are some scholars who argue that the shift in genre from the prose to poetry and back again is evidence of different authorship.[8] The general idea is that somewhere along the line a final compiler took a prose story and a poetry story and squashed them together to end up with what we currently have as the book of Job. The relationship between the prose and the poetry sections is a valid question. How do they relate? Why is Job so calm in one and so angry in the other? There have been several proposals over the years as to why and how the text looks the way it does. Some of those proposals require major rearrangements of the text. I suggest that a trauma-informed reading explains many of these perceived difficulties by simply recognizing the impact of trauma. Trauma represents an interruption in the flow of the survivor's story. It cannot be experienced in a linear, logical way, and it cannot be forgotten. Thus, the trauma remains on the to-do list, waiting to be addressed, always open. The past event continually intrudes on the present, acting, essentially, as a rupture in the chronology of the survivor's life. The missed encounter of the traumatic event becomes a lingering wound, dragging the past (where the trauma occurred) into the present, interrupting the chronology of the survivor's life story and creating a crisis of temporality. Past and present blur. This rupture in a survivor's life story gives the traumatic event an outside-of-time, out-of-reach quality that is noticeably out of place.

---

[8]See, for example, Zachary Margulies, "Oh That One Would Hear Me! The Dialogue of Job, Unanswered," *The Catholic Bible Quarterly* 82, no. 4 (October 2020): 582-604.

Just as the poetic section of the book of Job stands out as markedly different from, perhaps even an interruption in, the flow of the prose narrative, so too trauma occupies a different space in the story of the survivor's life, functioning as an interruption in their life narrative.

Why does all of this matter? As church leaders and fellow believers, we may be the ones trauma survivors turn to for comfort and support. Understanding how trauma impacts survivors and what makes it different from other types of experiences will enable us to come alongside those who are suffering and not be caught off-guard by a survivor's trauma response. The more we know about how trauma affects people and the normal and expected psychological and physiological responses that follow trauma, the better equipped we will be to provide the support system a survivor needs on their healing journey. Job's friends wanted to console and comfort Job, but they were unprepared for his response. They were not expecting the shards of broken glass that surrounded Job, and they did not know how to act as trusted listeners. In the end, their responses made the situation worse. As church leaders and believers, we desperately need to avoid inflicting further trauma on the survivors who turn to us for help because our delicate feet can't handle the broken glass.

UNMAKING THE WORLD

Another key thing we notice in Job 3 is the use of creation imagery in the poetry. This lays the groundwork for the continuing prevalence of creation imagery throughout the book of Job. It is also important to note the bookends of Job's use of creation imagery in Job 3 and YHWH's[9] use of creation imagery in Job 38–41. Creation language and imagery thus form a frame for the poetic section of text, similar to the overall prose framing of the totality of the text we discussed above. If you imagine a photograph that is matted and then framed, you get an idea

---

[9]Throughout this book I will use YHWH as the name of God.

of this double framing of the book of Job. The book opens with the prose prologue and closes with the prose epilogue so the prose framing is like the outside frame of the photograph. Then within that outside framing, creation imagery opens and closes the poetry section, so you have this second frame contained within the larger frame, like the matting that surrounds the photograph. Just as the prose framework in the prologue and epilogue draws attention to the messy poetic middle, the bookending of creation imagery in the text does the same thing.

Not only is the location of the creation imagery important, the content is as well. The creation imagery in Job 3 reveals a stunning de-creation metaphor that aligns strongly with the impact of trauma. Job's curse on the day of his birth is a powerful use of a reversal motif.[10] In a massive flip-flop, Job's creation language is not for creating, but for destroying. He is reversing creation in his language. The use of creation imagery in this de-creation metaphor becomes a thread that runs throughout the text and ultimately culminates in YHWH's speeches. This metaphor also draws attention to the larger de-creation that has occurred in Job's inner schematic world as a result of his traumatic experience. Job's world has, in effect, been de-created by his experience of trauma and he reflects this destruction in his words.

The de-creation metaphor begins early in Job 3. In the midst of his suffering and turmoil, Job curses the day of his birth and cries for darkness to cover it "Let that day be darkness!" (Job 3:4). There is an interesting parallel here with Genesis 1:3, "Then God said, 'Let there be light.'" God created the first day by calling for light, Job seeks to undo his first day by calling for darkness. What God created and ordered, Job is experiencing as uncreated and disordered. His world has been undone and unmade because of trauma. There is ample scholarly discussion on whether Job is intentionally trying to undo all of creation with a curse or whether he is engaging in a bit of intentional hyperbole,

---

[10]William Pohl, "Arresting God's Attention: The Rhetorical Intent and Strategies of Job 3," *Bulletin for Biblical Research* 28, no. 1 (2018): 10.

but what we can see in these verses is the depth of anguish Job is experiencing. Whether he wants to literally unmake the entire world is debatable, but his language points us to the destruction of *his* world.

The idea of the whole world falling apart makes excellent sense to someone who has experienced trauma. *Their* world has, in fact, fallen apart. It is in tatters all around them. To be stuck in the midst of a total collapse of everything you knew and depended on and then watch the rest of the world carry on as if nothing has happened is a strange place to be. As church leaders and comforters, it is important that we remain mindful of the far-reaching impact of trauma. When a wife discovers her husband's infidelity, it is not just a bad day. For her, her entire marriage has been shattered. It might have been a one-time mistake, it might have been years of betrayal and deception, but for the brokenhearted wife, the foundation of the most important relationship in her life has crumbled. The trauma of the affair reaches much further than the confession; it changes everything. For someone who receives a life-altering medical diagnosis or suffers a terrible accident the trauma is not just the bad news that needs to be processed. The questions and the fears the physical trauma raises go beyond medical procedures and doctor appointments. The survivor's sense of safety and security in the world has been shaken, their hopes for the future have been changed, perhaps irrevocably so. Their relationships have been altered. The levels of disruption in their cognitive schemas will vary from person to person, but trauma is never simple, and it always goes below the surface. There are certainly many more examples we can pull from here because trauma is not limited to a list of clearly defined events that we can review and say, "Oh yes, that is on the trauma list." Trauma is an individual response to an overwhelming event, which is why we have to be sensitive to each image bearer in our church or community and allow them to teach us about their experience.

For someone who is experiencing trauma, to watch the rest of the world keep turning as if nothing has happened is incredibly disorienting.

It's no wonder that Job calls down a curse on all of creation. His place in the world has changed. His perception of the world has changed. His sense of safety, security, purpose, and support is suddenly gone. For him, the world *has* ended, and he is just waiting for the formal destruction to catch up with what he already knows. This isn't narcissism or self-centeredness. It is a psychological and physiological inability to move past the experience. Remember, the event didn't get filed as it happened; it's still sitting in the survivor's mental inbox waiting for a place to go. The trauma survivor isn't being self-absorbed or continually living in the past. For them the trauma is still a present event, it is always in their inbox, so it feels like it is always happening. Their support system, their church, and their friends may process the event and put it in the past, but the survivor can't do that yet. It is our responsibility as trusted listeners and supporters to keep this temporal conundrum in mind. What is past for us, may be present for the trauma survivor. In the face of trauma, Job's orderly world dissolves into chaos, and the impact of this chaos is apparent in his metaphorical description of the undoing of the world.

Denial, Avoidance, and Change

One of the necessary elements of a trauma narrative is the story of the survivor's life prior to the traumatic event. Survivors need to be able to articulate what their life was like before the trauma struck. In the first two chapters of the book of Job, readers get a glimpse of Job's life prior to the series of losses he will soon endure. Readers are also given a glimpse into the reason behind Job's suffering, a piece of information that Job himself is never given. Following this baseline introduction to Job's life and character, trauma comes crashing in. The traumatic events occur in the prose section of the text, loss after loss, affliction after affliction. As Job's losses mount, his initial response is one that seems to be in line with his long-held schemas, as if he's still clinging to the fragments of his shattered window. It seems as though nothing has changed. And yet, everything in his life has changed.

The initial impact of the traumatic events on Job seems to be glossed over with little discussion in the text. After such a magnitude of suffering, Job's first response receives less space than the description of the losses. This initial minimal reaction is not surprising for two reasons. First, trauma survivors often try to hold on to their schemas even in the face of contradictory evidence. Second, there is the potential for denial and avoidance in the face of great loss. When everything falls apart, we may desperately try to hold on to what we know, what's comfortable and familiar, even when the circumstances tell us otherwise.

An impulse toward denial or avoidance is a natural and expected result of trauma.[11] Most people don't like it when their favorite grocery store changes its layout; imagine having to change your entire outlook on life, God, and the world. No one is ready for that kind of challenge, so we try to cling to what we're used to for as long as we can. Webb argues that a response of denial or avoidance is to be expected in trauma. She writes that a temporary phase of denial or avoidance

> may in fact be adaptive and necessary, as recently traumatized individuals are offered the opportunity to respond somewhat normally (albeit perhaps automatically) to the world around them, while they gather the internal strength and internal resources required to confront the challenges of the trauma before them.[12]

The idea here is that denial may be giving survivors the time and mental space they need to gather enough strength to face the massive healing work and rebuilding of their shattered world that will be required. Imagine you are out for walk and you suddenly find yourself at the foot of a long, steep staircase. You might stop for a moment to catch your breath and prepare for the climb before you take that first step. From this perspective, Job's first response is not necessarily inconsistent

---

[11]Webb, "The Book of Job," 163.

[12]Webb, "The Book of Job," 159. See also Ronnie Janoff-Bulman, *Shattered Assumptions: Towards a New Psychology of Trauma* (New York: The Free Press, 1992), 99-100 for a discussion of denial and emotional numbing in response to trauma.

with his later, more virulent response in the poetry section. It also warns us as comforters and trusted listeners that a person's first response to trauma will probably not be their last response. When we encounter someone in our churches or in our social circle who has faced something terrible, the death of a loved one, a medical diagnosis, financial loss, divorce, abuse, or anything that carries that kind of traumatic impact, their first response may be, like Job, one that sounds calm and controlled. They may look like they're holding it all together, like they have absorbed the shock and moved on. We may look at them and think, "Wow, what maturity they're showing, they must really know God and trust him so much." We see them seeming to cope and function without much difficulty, and so we assume that they've got this under control. They're good, so we can all talk about something else. And let's be honest we might even be relieved we don't have to deal with the messiness of it all. What these first two chapters of Job tell us is that a trauma survivor may be clinging to the fragments of their stained-glass window even as it shatters in their hand.

The task then falls to leaders and comforters to pay attention and watch for the potential shift. When a survivor's initial response fades and the reality of the trauma sets in, these same survivors who seemed so together and unflappable may have an abrupt change in their response. The problem occurs when we, as the support system, accepted their first response as their final response and moved on. The bystanders and witnesses, standing on the outside of the trauma, will move on much faster than the survivor who needs support. So, when that abrupt shift happens, when they, like Job, go from calm and quiet prose to riotous poetry (metaphorically speaking) we may be caught unawares. "Why are you saying this now? I thought you were over this? Haven't you moved on?" The result is, as we will see in Job's friends, a potential second injury to an already suffering survivor. The rejection, misunderstanding, or abandonment of a survivor's support system can be even more devastating than the original trauma.

So, what do we see in the book of Job regarding this changing response to trauma? Job's change between Job 2 and Job 3, from the
prose to the poetry, may be reflective of growing cognitive dissonance
as his experience collides with his beliefs. His experience has crashed
into his schemas and the schemas lost . . . the window is broken. Biblical scholar Carol Newsom highlights this relationship between the
shift in genres and the crisis in Job's belief system: "The juxtaposition
produces a character who has made a decisive break with a previous
worldview and identity."[13] Job's window is in pieces and suddenly he
sees it. He can't deny it or avoid it anymore. The wind and rain are
whipping through the open space with nothing left to hold it back.
The different reactions we see in Job in the prose and poetry are not
necessarily signs of disruptions in the text or the work of different
authors, but may, instead, be an important indicator of the depth of
the trauma Job is facing, the reality of the missed encounter nature of
trauma, and how the trauma impacts his worldview and theology.

When we encounter trauma survivors, people we love and care for,
it is understandable that we want to fix the situation as quickly as possible and get them to a better place. We may pull out all of our favorite
Bible verses and self-help tactics. We may tell them what we think they
should do or offer advice on what we would do in their situation. All of
this is (usually) well-intentioned and comes from a place of sincerely
wanting them to feel better. But the reality is, we have to embrace the
bad before we can embrace better. The pain of trauma cannot be bandaged and forgotten. It is a deep wound that impacts the very core of a
person's beliefs and coping skills. As trauma survivors we need to allow
ourselves the grace to understand that we don't understand. We may
have to stand in the wind and the rain of our broken window for a while.
As pastors, church leaders, and fellow believers we need to be okay with
survivors not being okay, and not being okay for what may be a long

---

[13]Carol Newsom, *The Book of Job: A Contest of Moral Imaginations* (New York: Oxford University
Press, 2003), 26.

time. Both of those are hard, believe me, I know. The truth is that suffering is scary. It is scary for those of us going through it, and it is scary for those of us witnessing it. Suffering is uncomfortable, alarming, and terrifying. It strikes at the heart of our sense of security and safety. It forces us to look at the unpredictability and unfairness of the world. How often have we tried to quickly comfort someone out of their pain so *we* can feel better? But that is part of the ministry of presence, being with someone and not trying to fix them, not forcing forgiveness, not pressuring a happy ending. Can we simply sit with them in the midst of their pain and be okay with them not being okay for as long as it takes?

LESSONS LEARNED

- Silence can be an important part in trauma healing. When we don't have the words to describe our experience, sometimes silence is all we have.

- Job's changing response from the prose chapters to the poetry section may be explained by understanding the way trauma ruptures a survivor's life story. This is reflected in the way the poetry ruptures the prose narrative in the book of Job.

- A trauma survivor's first response to a trauma-inducing event may not be their final response. Changing perspectives is normal and expected.

REFLECTION QUESTIONS

- As a trauma survivor, how does this chapter impact your view of what you have been through and how you have dealt with it?

- How does understanding trauma as a rupture impact how you view those who have experienced a trauma-inducing event, including suffering you have endured?

- Does the idea of the poetry acting as a rupture in the text change how you view the book of Job?

THREE

THE MINISTRY
OF PRESENCE

A FEW YEARS AGO, I read a story in David Platt's book *Something Needs to Change* that deeply affected me.[1] In the book, Platt shares about his trip hiking in the Himalayas. One day, on their way out of the mountains, he and his group encountered a strange sight. A man was sitting on a chair in the middle of the trail surrounded by two other men. As Platt watched, one of the men knelt down while the other helped lift the man in the chair onto the kneeling man's back. The men then proceeded to carry the man down the trail. The man in the chair had broken his legs in a remote village high up in the mountains. Without medical care, he was certain to die. His two friends strapped him to a chair and took turns carrying him down the mountains to the bus station where he would be able to go to the nearest doctor. The image made a deep impression on Platt and me as well. These two men saw their friend in need, and they spent days carrying him on their backs down a treacherous mountain trail so he could get

---

[1]David Platt, *Something Needs to Change: A Call to Make Your Life Count in a World of Urgent Need* (Colorado Springs, CO: Multnomah, 2019), 169.

medical care. It still makes me teary-eyed to think of that kind of friendship and compassion, and it breaks my heart to know that so often the church, rather than carrying the wounded, chooses instead to leave the broken behind.

Trauma research teaches us that when we are in the midst of suffering and hardship, the people we choose to confide in and turn to for help will have a significant impact on our healing. Whether that impact will be either positive or negative is the big question. In my unbridled optimism, I choose to believe that most people do not intend to cause additional harm. Most of us simply don't know how to respond to trauma in a healthy, life-giving way. We turn to platitudes because we don't know what else to say. We tell people to forgive, move on, and let it go because sitting in the ashes of their grief and pain is too uncomfortable for us. We think, in our very best of intentions, that the key to healing is getting a survivor back to normal as quickly as possible. We tell them to forgive, forget, and forge ahead so they can get back to "normal life" and put this whole messy thing in the past. Or we tell them to turn the mess into a message, turn the test into a testimony, find the purpose in their pain so they can give glory to God. All of that may be true, but the right message at the wrong time is still the wrong message. While I believe this type of counsel and support comes, usually, from a good place, it runs the risk of inflicting greater pain and secondary trauma on a survivor who may not be ready to forgive, forget, and forge ahead.

On the other side of this coin are people who respond poorly to a trauma survivor out of fear. Trauma is scary, not just for the person going through it, but for those who witness it as well. C. L. Seow's translation of one particular verse in Job addresses this reality. Job is speaking to the three friends and says, "You see trauma and you fear" (Job 6:21).[2] When we witness trauma, when we witness someone

---

[2]C. L. Seow, *Job 1–21: Interpretation and Commentary* (Grand Rapids, MI: Eerdmans, 2013), 91.

else's suffering, it naturally brings up questions for us. What does that person's trauma mean? Why is it happening? What does it mean for my position and my reputation? What does it mean for our church? What will people think of us? What does it mean for how I view God? If something so horrible happened to her, could it happen to me as well? Those are all questions that may spring up for a witness. The ramifications and ripples of someone else's trauma has the potential to deeply affect those around the survivor as well. That is not a bad thing. We are, after all, relational creatures. We are made for community and relationship. Unfortunately, fear and uncertainty can cause us to respond poorly and make the trauma worse. A second injury to a trauma survivor, inflicted by the very community they turned to for help, can be worse than the initial traumatic event.[3] How we steward someone else's pain matters. This is especially true in the church because the church is meant to be a safe place. It is meant to be a place where the broken and wounded can find healing. The church is not a building or an institution or a platform to be protected. The church is people, the body of Christ, each and every man, woman, and child is a part of the body that needs to be cared for, and every little c local church should reflect that big C Church reality.

Pastors, leaders, and fellow believers have a significant responsibility when it comes to hearing stories of pain and trauma. Not just in terms of confidentiality and safety, but also in terms of speaking words that reflect the heart of God. When a pastor fails a trauma survivor, it is easy for the survivor to confuse a person's rejection of them with God's rejection. A pastor who mishandles a survivor's pain has the potential to inflict secondary trauma that can impact the survivor's relationship with God, the church, and their community. It is one of the reasons why church leaders need to be able to recognize signs of trauma, respond with safety and trust, and also know when

---

[3] Ronnie Janoff-Bulman, *Shattered Assumptions: Towards a New Psychology of Trauma* (New York: The Free Press, 1992), 147.

to refer a survivor to professional mental health care. God cares deeply for every one of his people. Our brokenness does not make us less worthy of his love. Our pain and trauma is not an inconvenience to God, and it should not be viewed as an inconvenience to the church that needs to be solved and forgotten as quickly as possible so the church can look good. Ministering to the broken and hurting is not an inconvenience, it is a vital part of the church's role in this broken world.

This issue of how a poor response to trauma can inflict further injury is evident in the book of Job in the words and actions of his friends. When Job's friends, Eliphaz, Bildad, and Zophar, heard about Job's suffering, they traveled to see him and comfort and console him. What started out as a well-intentioned course of action to comfort a grieving friend quickly devolved into a theological debate and name calling. However, before we pile on Job's friends and point out all the ways they goofed up, let's acknowledge first that these three men sat with Job in the ash heap for seven days. They sat beside their friend in his grief and loss. They didn't say anything, they simply sat with him and let him know that he was not alone.

There is something truly beautiful in this ministry of presence. Job suffered the loss of his children, his wealth, his reputation, his influence in the community, and his health. And while Job is not an Israelite, his skin disease may have led his community to consider him unclean. He ended up alone on the ash heap outside of town. The losses he suffered may have made others wonder if he was cursed or if he had committed a terrible sin to deserve such severe punishment from God. Job was alone in his misery, suffering a terrible disease, reduced to poverty, and yet, these three friends sat with him. They tore their clothes and dropped to the dirt beside Job. They did not pick him up, dust him off, and tell him to get back out there. They sat with him, right there in the ashes and ruins and gave him the gift of their presence. Throughout this book I will often refer to the ashes as the site of pain and trauma. It is true that the book of Job only references the ash heap twice, but it is an important element in the text. The entire poetic middle of the book takes place on the ash heap. So even though it doesn't get mentioned often, it is always there, and it makes a great metaphor for trauma.

This simple act of being willing to sit with someone in their pain is monumental. Most of us run from pain. We don't like needles, we don't like being too hot or too cold, we don't like failing or doing something embarrassing, so we do all we can to avoid those situations. Seeing someone in pain and not knowing how to fix it can be equally scary, and the temptation for many of us is to avoid the situation. Yet, instead of running from Job's pain, his friends came to him. They sat with him, they stayed with him. They didn't offer quick fixes or easy solutions (yet). Their presence was their greatest ministry to him. Even though they may mess it up in the coming chapters, in that first moment, Job's friends demonstrate the compassion of presence.

The willingness of Job's friends to sit in the ashes raises an interesting interpretive question about the connection between their actions and a mourning ritual. There is no academic agreement on whether the seven days of silence in Job is an intentional example of a mourning ritual, but the potential has been noted.[4] The connection goes back to Genesis 50:10 where Joseph and those with him observed seven days of mourning for his father, Jacob. Though arguments about how the friends' actions in the book of Job and Jewish ritual mourning may be connected are interesting, attempting to discern which tradition came first and whether one intentionally built on the other is speculative at best. However, the potential connection has

---

[4]See, for example, John E. Hartley, *The Book of Job* (Grand Rapids, MI: Eerdmans, 1988), 86; David Clines, *Job 1–20* (Grand Rapids, MI: Harper Collins, 1989), 63; Seow, *Job 1–21*, 299; Samuel Balentine, *Job* (Macon, GA: Smyth & Helwys, 2006), 68. Seow points out that in "Jewish tradition, comforters are to remain silent until the mourner speaks, but that Talmudic tradition may have been derived from this passage in Job" (Seow, *Job 1–21*, 309). If the Joban tradition predates the Talmudic tradition, it is possible that these seven days were not an established mourning ritual but were recorded in the book of Job and later adopted as a Jewish mourning ritual.

something significant to offer in a trauma-informed reading of the book of Job as it brings us to the issue of grief. Grief has an important role to play in the experience of trauma. There is grieving to be done when trauma hits. A traumatic experience may represent the death of something. A marriage may suddenly be dead due to adultery. A church community's betrayal may mean the loss of community, ministry, and friendships. A medical diagnosis may represent the death of a previous lifestyle or the death of future hopes and dreams. Sexual assault, spiritual abuse, physical abuse, financial devastation, illness: the list goes on and on of different things that trauma may steal from a survivor. Grief acknowledges these losses and makes space for mourning. As both survivors and comforters, it is necessary for us to recognize the grief that comes with trauma. There is mourning to be done. What is lost deserves to be mourned. Judith Herman notes this in her work on trauma and the importance of remembrance and mourning.[5] Telling the story of our experience can provide survivors the opportunity to name, acknowledge, and grieve what we have lost.

Trusted Listeners

Trauma can be an isolating and lonely experience. A survivor can feel utterly alone in the midst of their suffering. The reality is that this may not be a feeling at all; it may be fact. Trauma has a tendency to push people away, whether by the survivor's choice or because the situation is too uncomfortable for others. We may say we are giving a survivor space, but in reality, we may be giving ourselves space because we don't know what to say. We may be trying to avoid the ashes. Talking about trauma can bring people together or drive them apart. Trauma survivors may find themselves isolated and struggling to heal without any social support. We see this illustrated in the book of Job when Job is alone on the ash heap. His experience of trauma has set him apart

---

[5]Judith Herman, *Trauma and Recovery: The Aftermath of Violence—from Domestic Abuse to Political Terror* (New York: Basic Books), 175.

and distanced him from his community. He occupies a liminal space, a place of neither here nor there. He is no longer the man he was, but he is not yet the man he will become after the trauma. He is in a transitional phase, a man without a place. His physical isolation ends when his friends arrive and sit with him in the ash heap, but once the words start to flow, Job's separateness will become obvious again as he and the three friends discover how far apart they are in their beliefs about Job's suffering.

After seven days of silence, Job launches into the poetry of Job 3. His curse against the day of his birth and his use of the de-creation metaphor points to the shattering of his worldview and his inner schemas. He cries out from a place of trauma and suffering, and his friends are stunned. We can only speculate about what his friends thought Job would say when he finally broke his silence. What we do know is that they were not expecting this. Job's words shock his friends, and their reaction sets the tone for the coming contentious debate in the dialogue cycles. They cannot accept Job's perspective. His claims that his losses and suffering are unwarranted and unjust is too much for their theological worldview. Job's version of the events is threatening to them. It challenges *their* fundamental assumptions, and they cannot embrace that. In order to protect their worldview and their understanding of God, his friends have to prove that Job is wrong. Because if Job is right . . . *their* whole world will turn upside down, too.

Now, again, before we pile on Job's friends and point out what a terrible job they did, we need to pause for a moment. First, they were the only ones who showed up. These were the friends who heard about Job's suffering and did something about it. They deserve acknowledgment for that. Second, we also need to acknowledge that we are all wounded comforters. We all bring our own pain, our own baggage, and our own scars to every conversation. I can't pretend to know what was going on with the friends, but I do know they were deeply entrenched in a Retribution Principle worldview. When Job challenged that theology, he was challenging the very foundation of their beliefs. That was probably terrifying. So, while we're going to look honestly at where things went sideways with the friends, I want to be as compassionate to them as I can be.

With that said, what we see in the friends' reactions is a failure to act as trusted listeners. A trusted listener is someone who can listen to a survivor's story without agenda and without judgment. This listening other provides the survivor with a safe place to process their trauma and work through what it means and how it has affected them. A trusted listener is a vital element in trauma resolution and healing. Job's friends were able to demonstrate compassion and support by their presence, but they stumble when it comes to listening. They cannot hear and accept Job's story because of the implications it has for them. Trauma can be threatening. In order to alleviate their own discomfort and protect their own assumptions, the friends must explain Job's trauma in a way that maintains their theological agenda. While there is value in wise counsel, and it will always be necessary to speak truth in dark circumstances, what we see here is the imposition of an agenda, in this case a theological agenda. It is an imposition that causes further harm to a trauma survivor in an attempt to preserve the status quo.

Before we delve into the theological agenda of the friends, let's take a brief moment to address the ramifications of this idea of imposing an agenda. In the book of Job, Job's friends are pushing a theological agenda, one that will explain away Job's suffering as a just and deserved punishment for his sins. However, the idea of imposing an agenda on a trauma survivor's experience goes beyond just theological categories. As pastors and church leaders, we can impose a business agenda on a trauma survivor, putting the reputation or business platform of the church ahead of a trauma survivor's needs. As witnesses to trauma, we may impose relational agendas on a

survivor in an attempt to preserve family, friend, or network relationships. As comforters we may impose social agendas in order to preserve or press our understanding of authority, marriage, or gender
roles. The specific agenda can take many forms and it may not even
be a conscious attempt at undermining the trauma survivor, but the
bottom line is the same. Sometimes, as trusted listeners, pastors, and
comforters, this imposition is unintentional. These agendas are simply
so much a part of our belief systems and worldview that we may not
recognize that our impulse to provide an answer is really an attempt,
well-intentioned as it may be, to impose our perspective of the situation on a wounded survivor. We may be so sure that we understand
what's happened that we focus on getting the survivor to accept our
view of the situation. We may even have a whole pile of Bible verses
to back up our opinion. The difficulty is that the imposition of an
agenda, no matter the motivation, asks a survivor to accept *our* view
of the situation. It runs the risk of silencing the trauma survivor's
voice and depriving them of the necessary opportunity to express and
understand their own experience.

What we see in the book of Job, and what applies to the church, is
the ripple effect of trauma. A trauma survivor's experience can have an
impact on those around the survivor and on those with whom the
survivor chooses to share their story. Trauma feels, and often is, isolating, but its effects can reach into the lives of those who surround the
survivor. This recognition of the ripple effect of Job's traumatic experience is illustrated in the text. When Job begins to question everything
he thought he knew about God, creation, and the order of the world,
the friends cannot support him. The friends know Job, they know his
reputation for righteousness and blamelessness, yet they refuse to
question their understanding of the doctrine of retribution even when
they see the suffering of a man whom they know to be righteous. Their
stubborn devotion to their particular understanding of God leads them
to immediately discount Job's view of his experience. (Is anyone else

thinking of social media debates at the moment?) The friends do not give Job a safe place to work through his experience, instead they attempt to impose their understanding of the events on Job. When Job refuses to go along with it, the verbal fireworks commence.

Let's explore both the rigidity of the friends' cognitive conservatism and their increasing vitriol toward what they perceive as an unrepentant Job. Eliphaz is the first friend to speak after Job's outburst in Job 3. His initial words to Job are tentative and even gentle.

> If one ventures a word with you, will you be offended?
>   But who can keep from speaking?
> See, you have instructed many;
>   you have strengthened the weak hands.
> Your words have supported those who were stumbling,
>   and you have made firm the feeble knees.
> But now it has come to you, and you are impatient;
>   it touches you, and you are dismayed.
> Is not your fear of God your confidence
>   and the integrity of your ways your hope? (Job 4:2-6)

But this congenial tone is gone by his final speech to Job in the third dialogue cycle.

> Is it for your piety that he reproves you
>   and enters into judgment with you?
> Is not your wickedness great?
>   There is no end to your iniquities.
> For you have exacted pledges from your family for no reason
>   and stripped the naked of their clothing.
> You have given no water to the weary to drink,
>   and you have withheld bread from the hungry.
> The powerful possess the land,
>   and the favored live in it.
> You have sent widows away empty-handed,
>   and the arms of the orphans you have crushed.

Therefore snares are around you,
  and sudden terror overwhelms you,
or darkness so that you cannot see;
  a flood of water covers you. (Job 22:4-11)

As this example from Eliphaz shows, the dialogue between Job and his friends devolves into insults as the two conflicting understandings of Job's experience are set against each other. Job cannot reconcile his traumatic experience with his previously held schemas and the friends cannot compromise on their fundamental beliefs. Job is working through the breakdown of his inner schemas. He is talking through it, venting, and trying to find an explanation that works, but his friends fail in their role as trusted listeners. Their devotion to their own perspective and their inability to engage in the same type of searching Job exhibits renders them incapable of functioning as trusted listeners. Essentially, they are more committed to their agenda than they are to the wounded person before them.

Such a statement is not intended to paint the friends as cruel or heartless. They were, in fact, the only people in the text who joined Job in his suffering, sat beside him, and gave him their presence in the midst of his pain. It is, however, important to note that within the context of trauma resolution, the role of the trusted listener is essential. As Job attempts to work through his confusion, he needs a listening other to receive the story. The friends' focus on preserving their retributive worldview and their pressure on Job to accept their explanation and hurry up and repent removes their ability to function objectively in the role of trusted listeners. In other words, they are not listening to learn about Job's perspective; they are listening to respond with their own opinion.

Job's shattered worldview threatens the friends' beliefs about suffering and how God operates. If the friends acknowledge the possibility that Job is right they would also have to recognize the fragility and potential falsity of their own deeply help schemas. If Job is right that suffering can be unjust and unfair, what would that mean for them? As Bill Kynes describes it, using Bildad as an example, "Bildad simply cannot believe that God would treat a godly man the way Job has been treated. That would throw the whole moral fabric of the universe into disarray; the very foundations, the rocks on which he has built his life, would be demolished."[6] The friends cannot engage in this kind of thinking without risking the shattering of their own assumptions. So they can't listen. It becomes a "dialogue of the deaf."[7] Instead of acting as trusted listeners, the friends focus on pressuring Job to accept their perspective. Job's friends confuse comfort with instruction. Instead of being able to listen well to Job's story, they see his confusion, sorrow, and suffering as a time for a lesson in theology. They seek to instruct Job on how he should react, how he should behave, what he should do. We see this, for example in Eliphaz's words, "As for me, I would seek God, and to God I would commit my cause" (Job 5:8). And this is in his very first response to Job. Eliphaz immediately tells him, "Hey, if it were me, this is what I would do." He is not there to listen and learn, he is there to instruct, and it is in that intentional imposition of his perspective that Eliphaz fails as a trusted listener and the other friends follow in his footsteps.

And so, Job is isolated from his support community, both physically as he sits on the ash heap, and psychologically as his attempts to explain his trauma are dismissed, denied, and denigrated by the very people he trusted to listen to him. Thus, the friends are not merely "miserable comforters" (Job 16:2), they also represent the failure of others to provide the necessary support for trauma survivors to work through their experience. "In a familiar experience for trauma survivors, Job feels himself as cut off from others, set apart by his

---

[6]Bill Kynes and Will Kynes, *Wrestling with Job: Defiant Faith in the Face of Suffering* (Downers Grove, IL: IVP Academic, 2022), 68.
[7]Gustavo Gutiérrez, *On Job: Suffering and God Talk* (Maryknoll, NY: Orbis, 1996), 23.

experience of victimization that no one seems to understand, that everyone wants to justify or whitewash."[8]

What does this mean for us as comforters who come face-to-face with trauma survivors? There are several important takeaways in this brief discussion of the friends. First, the ministry of presence. We cannot underestimate the importance of sitting with someone in the ashes of their experience. Job's friends heard about his suffering and went to him. They didn't hear about his losses and shake their heads sadly and send their "prayers for a speedy recovery." They invested their time, their energy, and their money to travel to him. Please take note of that . . . Job's friends went to him. They didn't send a text or leave a voicemail: "I'm here if you need anything. Just let me know." The reality is trauma survivors may not know what they need. Their whole world has been shaken and upended. How can we expect them to put together an itemized list of needs? When we expect trauma survivors to tell us, their support system, what they need, we risk putting an additional burden on their already struggling hearts. We are asking them to tell us what to do, to give us an assignment; we are asking them to take care of our need to feel useful. Job's friends may have eventually caused more harm than good with their words, but in those initial seven days, they took the initiative. They went to Job. When they didn't know what to do, they simply sat with him. When others ran from Job, these friends drew closer to him. That is our first lesson: we must be willing to go to the hurting, seek them out, and get dirty in the ashes.

Second, we must learn the lesson of listening. When survivors begin to process their traumatic experience, they will need a listening other. This role can be, and often should be, filled by a professional therapist, but pastoral counseling and the wisdom and compassionate care of friends also have a vital part to play in healing from trauma. A

---

[8]Cataldo, "I Know That My Redeemer Lives," 799.

survivor needs both. There is wisdom in knowing when to refer survivors to appropriate professional care. That does not take away from the role of the pastor or friends, it is simply an act of responsible stewardship and leadership. The listening other, whether a therapist, a pastor, or a friend, has an important and necessary role in the resolution and healing of trauma. It is a role that must be undertaken with compassion and patience. Job's friends were unable to separate their theological agenda from their care for their friend. Job's experience threatened their worldview, so they tried to shut him down. They did not listen, they debated. They could not give Job the freedom to talk through his experience because they were too busy telling him what they thought he should do. Trusted listeners need the maturity, objectivity, and compassion to set their own agenda aside and allow the survivor to talk without fear of censure. It is not an easy task, but it is a necessary one. It also offers us, as trusted listeners, witnesses, and leaders, the opportunity to learn in humility. Just as survivors may learn something new about God, his character, his creation, and themselves, as they walk through their healing, we, as comforters, can learn as well. And we cannot be in a place to learn if we think our only role in the journey is to teach the survivor how to move on.

There is always space for a trusted listener to address potentially destructive ideas. A survivor who worries that God has forsaken them or hates them needs to hear that God is faithful, God does love them, and God will never abandon them. But there is an important difference between sharing biblical counsel in a way that allows the survivor to hear it, examine it, and decide for themselves how it fits in their shattered world and telling a survivor what to think. Remember, trauma healing involves rebuilding the entire shattered window. Each piece has to be individually put in place. We cannot tell a survivor what their window must look like. Our task is to help them pick up the pieces one by one and support them as they assemble the pieces into a new mosaic.

LESSONS LEARNED

- Trauma survivors often feel isolated and alienated from their community. Being present with someone who is suffering is ministry. As comforters, we can take the initiative and reach out to trauma survivors.

- Being a trusted listener involves listening to someone's story without judgment or agenda. It is listening to learn instead of listening to reply.

- Survivors need the space to process their trauma in their own way, without comforters imposing an explanation or course of action on them.

REFLECTION QUESTIONS

- What does the ministry of presence look like? How can we implement this in our church community?

- When was the last time someone came alongside you in a time of pain and supported you without judgment or agenda? What did that look like? What do you remember about it?

- How would you describe Job's friends right now? Do they remind you of anyone, maybe even yourself?

FOUR

TALKING ABOUT TRAUMA

ONE OF THE STRIKING FEATURES of the book of Job is the heavy emphasis on dialogue. There is a lot of talking in this text, and I mean *a lot* of talking. Between the bookends of the prose prologue and epilogue, there is dialogue. So much dialogue. In fact, the vast majority of the book of Job is written, not only in poetry, but in dialogue form. Once Job begins to speak in Job 3, there is no end to the talking. Job and the three friends go round and round, and just when you think there's nothing left to say, another character, Elihu, shows up and joins the conversation. Finally, YHWH appears in the whirlwind and starts talking. What we find in this middle section of the book of Job is multiple rounds of dialogue . . . dialogue that also happens to be poetry. This is not a simple, straightforward conversation where Job speaks, a friend speaks, YHWH speaks, and we all go home. It is an intentional and repetitious cycle of dialogues. While there is some scholarly debate on how exactly we should classify and organize these chapters, the general consensus is that the author intended to create a structured dialogue format. Dialogue is a vital element in the text, and it points us to the importance of talking in the process of trauma healing.

Since we are relational beings, most of us like to talk about our lives. The good, the bad, and everything else. Have you ever had a rotten day and you just needed to vent about it? From spilling your morning coffee to the traffic on the way to work to the coworker who stole your lunch (again) to your boss adding to your already overwhelming to-do list to the person who cut you off on the drive home to coming home to an overflowing toilet. It's a no-good, rotten day. So, you find your spouse or call a friend and just pour it all out, barely taking a breath, until you've described every last horrible detail of the day. There is something about talking through the frustrations and pains and enraging aspects of life that helps ease the ache in our heart. Sometimes we have a sticky problem we're trying to work through, and we just need someone to listen to our train of thought. In my home, I'm famous for doing this when I'm writing a novel and get stuck on a plot point. "Okay, the building is on fire, but I need the hero to be able to get the kids out. How is he supposed to run through fire? Is there a separate part of the building? Maybe the sprinklers come on. . . ." On and on I will go, talking through fictional catastrophes over dinner and my family will listen and occasionally offer suggestions, but mostly they listen while I talk through it and find a solution. There is a great blessing in having someone who is willing to just listen.

It's not just the bad stuff we want to share with people we love and trust. When we get a promotion or adopt a puppy or find the love of our life, that kind of joy begs to be shared. We want to tell a friend all about it, so we have someone to share in our happiness. It is in the sharing of experiences that we not only receive validation for our experiences—doesn't something suddenly seem more real once you tell someone else about it?— we also build and deepen our relationships. When we have a trusted person to share our experiences with, when we have a place where we can unload all of the pent-up aggravations, those burdens become lighter. The freedom in being able to give words to our experiences and express the feelings those experiences cause and then share those words with

someone else brings healing. Part of the isolating and lonely consequences of trauma comes from (1) not being able to put the experience
into words and (2) not being able to share it freely with another person.

The use of dialogue within the book of Job is reflective of the important role dialogue plays for us in the processing and integration of a
traumatic experience. While the modern psychological language of
trauma theory and trauma processing was certainly unknown to the
author of the book of Job, the human experience of trauma was present
in the ancient world. A quick skim of the Hebrew Bible testifies to that.
The Bible is filled with stories of war, famine, exile, rape, starvation, and
slavery. The ancient writers recognized trauma. They experienced it, witnessed it, and at times, they inflicted it. What we understand now, and
are continuing to discover, about the importance of talking and sharing
in trauma resolution gives us interesting insights into the book of Job.
First, we see the literary choice to move the story forward through dialogue. The author does not describe the interactions between Job and his
friends using narrative description. "Job began speaking, wishing he had
never been born. His friend Eliphaz was offended by such talk and told
Job that he needed to stop saying such things and trust God." Instead, the
author uses dialogue to propel the story. The author doesn't describe the
situation to us, the author lets Job and his friends tell us in their own
words. Second, we see the ongoing development of Job's thought, albeit
in a twisty-turny, nonlinear fashion, throughout the course of the dialogue. As Job works through his trauma, his perspective changes until
we end up at the conclusion of the book with Job being able to leave the
ash heap and rejoin his community. There is healing in the dialogue.

This connection between talking and the healing of trauma was
noted in the earliest days of modern psychoanalysis and trauma research, though it hadn't been named "trauma research" yet. It was even
called the "talking cure."[1] Herman notes that these early researchers

---

[1] Judith Herman, *Trauma and Recovery: The Aftermath of Violence—from Domestic Abuse to Political Terror* (New York: Basic Books), 12.

and practitioners discovered that a patient's symptoms of hysteria could be lessened when the patient was able to put the traumatic memories and the feelings associated with those memories into words.[2] Talking about a traumatic event gives survivors space to examine, consider, and process the event.[3] The heavy emphasis on dialogue in the book of Job reflects this need to verbalize and discuss trauma as a part of the healing process. This teaches us two things. First, as survivors, talking about what we've been through with a trusted listener can be a big part of our healing process. Second, as comforters, we need to be prepared for trauma survivors to have a pressing need to talk. It's true that it may take a while for them to reach a point where they are ready to talk about their experiences, remember Job's friends sat in silence with him for seven days before the dialogue started, but when the dam opens, we must be ready to receive those words in a supportive and life-giving way. That is where Job's friends failed.

JOB AND HIS THREE FRIENDS

When writing this section, I initially put the word *friends* in the heading in quotation marks because, in the end, Job's friends didn't seem like very good friends. But then I took the quotation marks out because I realized that it is because these three men were his friends that their words to Job were so hurtful. If it had been strangers on the street who told Job that his suffering was his fault and that he needed to repent so God would bless him again, Job might not have taken the words to heart. It was the fact that these words came from people he trusted, people that were his friends and his support system, that made the words so painful. They knew Job, they knew his life, his family, his deeds. Job counted them among his friends, his community. It is the betrayal of his *friends*, not the scorn of strangers, that compounds his trauma.

---

[2] Herman, *Trauma and Recovery*, 12.
[3] Ronnie Janoff-Bulman, *Shattered Assumptions: Towards a New Psychology of Trauma* (New York: The Free Press, 1992), 108.

It is also worth noting here that, as readers, we may have an impulse to dismiss the friends right off the bat. Having read the entirety of the book of Job and knowing how it ends, we may be tempted to toss the friends and everything they say in the trash bin right from the start. However, the friends play an important role in the book of Job. What we see in the dialogues between Job and the friends is Job's shattered window coming into direct conflict with the intact and unchallenged windows of the friends. Job's glasses have been broken but the friends still expect him to see the world through the same lenses they use. When Job expresses his pain, confusion, and shaken assumptions about the world, his words challenge the beliefs of the friends. This clash leads to conflict. Job can't believe what the friends believe anymore and when he says that, in occasionally shocking and graphic ways, the friends push back. The friends fail as trusted listeners because they are focused on trying to get Job back in line. They want him to get back onboard with the Retribution Principle program and stop questioning what they believe is true about God, the world, and creation.

We don't know why the friends are so committed to their worldview that they cannot listen compassionately to what Job is saying. The text doesn't give any clues about their background or what pain they may be carrying that leads them to such a stubborn stance. The friends give us an example of what not to do as comforters, but they also give us a compassionate warning about how we, as comforters, must be aware of our own pain and the beliefs we bring to the table. We are all wounded in our way. To be helpful and healthy comforters, we need to be aware of our own scars and seek our own healing where we need it.

Thus, we cannot simply dismiss the friends as bad theologians and poor comforters, though they might be. The friends function as necessary dialogue partners for Job's trauma processing, and they also serve as illustrations of the impact of trauma on social relationships. They demonstrate the potential for further wounding when a survivor's community fails to provide the care and support a survivor needs. As we strive to learn from the book of Job and apply these insights to our own ministry contexts, whether that is in our church, work, or in our friendships, we need to hold both of these truths in tension. The friends are not examples for us to follow, but their function in the text helps us see and understand how Job is processing and working through his trauma.

Looking at the interactions between Job and his three friends, scholars often note the repetitive structure of these conversations. These conversations are often referred to as "dialogue cycles." While there is some debate about the nature of the dialogue cycles—who speaks first, how many cycles are there, whether there are portions of the dialogue that have been mixed up in manuscript transmission— the traditional approach is to see three dialogue cycles between Job and his three friends while Elihu and YHWH are usually treated as separate dialogues.[4] If we look at the initial conversations as three dialogue cycles what we have is this:

Cycle One: Eliphaz speaks (chapter 4)[5]
                Job speaks (Job 5–7)
                Bildad speaks (Job 8)
                Job speaks (Job 9–10)
                Zophar speaks (Job 11)
                Job speaks (Job 12–14)

Cycle Two: Eliphaz speaks (Job 15)
                Job speaks (Job 16–17)
                Bildad speaks (Job 18)
                Job speaks (Job 19)
                Zophar speaks (Job 20)
                Job speaks (Job 21)

---

[4]See, for example, David J. A. Clines, *Job 1–20* (Grand Rapids, MI: HarperCollins Christian, 1989), lvii–lix.

[5]I am not including Job's monologue in Job 3 as part of the first dialogue cycle. There are good arguments both for including it as the first part of the first dialogue cycle and good arguments for treating it as its own monologue. I have chosen to follow Longman's position here. Tremper Longman, III, *Job*, Baker Commentary on the Old Testament Wisdom and Psalms (Grand Rapids, MI: Baker Academic, 2012), 108.

Cycle Three: Eliphaz speaks (Job 22)
Job speaks (Job 23–24)
Bildad speaks (Job 25)
Job speaks (Job 26–27)

There is a lot to unpack just in the structure of these dialogue cycles, so hang with me. What is immediately striking is the orderliness of the first two cycles and the disorder of the third cycle. Some scholars see the breakdown of the third dialogue cycle, including Bildad's very short speech (only five verses) and the absence of any words at all from Zophar as evidence of manuscript corruption.[6] However, the formal structure of the dialogue cycles and the apparent disintegration of this structure in the third cycle has a powerful resonance with trauma and trauma processing. Trauma, as we have seen, is by nature chaotic and disorganized. It is the rock smashing through a window. The pieces fall to the ground in a random mess with little rhyme or reason. Trauma smashes through our lives with the same kind of shattering. Before we can start processing and understanding the event, we need to bring some structure to the mess. It's like dumping a jigsaw puzzle onto a table. Before we can start assembling all the pieces, we need to at least turn them all face up. This need to bring order to the chaos of trauma, and to bring organization to the disjointed experience of the traumatic event, is illustrated in the structure of the dialogue cycles in the book of Job.

In the first two dialogue cycles, Job and his friends engage in formal, structured dialogue. There are rules. Everyone takes a turn speaking. Even though their words get progressively more strident and snarky, there is structure here. Job's life is in chaos, as we see in his de-creation cry in his monologue in chapter three, but the author is imposing structure on the disorganized circumstances by using a formal dialogue format. This imposition of structure on a chaotic event is reminiscent of

---

[6]For example, Clines argues the original manuscript has suffered transmission errors and because of those errors, sections of the third dialogue cycle have been attributed to the speakers incorrectly. He suggests for an extensive restructuring of the third dialogue cycle in order to maintain the symmetry of the first two cycles (Clines, *Job 21–37*, 663).

the book of Lamentations. In Lamentations, the chaos and trauma of a terrible event, most likely the destruction of Jerusalem by the Babylonians, is recounted in a series of acrostic poems, a style that has strict rules and a formal format.[7] It is an attempt to organize the chaos of the event by telling it in an organized, structured way. Similarly, we see this type of imposition of order on chaos in the book of Job in the formal structure of the first two dialogue cycles. However, by the third dialogue cycle, the structured format has gone out the broken window and disorganization returns. Bildad's speech is cut short, and Zophar doesn't even get to say a word. This third dialogue cycle has disintegrated into chaos.

From a trauma-informed perspective, this makes sense. At this point, the dialogue between Job and his three friends has reached an impasse. The friends' attempts to convince Job that his suffering is just punishment for sin and that he needs to repent have failed as Job maintains steadfast adherence to his innocence and his claims that his suffering is unjust. The conflict has led to acrimony and insults. There is no resolution to Job's trauma here. His friends have failed as comforters, he has found himself isolated from his community, and his words have landed on deaf ears. It is perhaps no wonder that the dialogue between Job and his friends breaks down. As Seow comments, "Instead of being a result of corruptions in the process of transmission, one might rather view the third cycle as literary representations of the state of the conversation between Job and his friends."[8] If the first two dialogue cycles represented an attempt to bring order to the chaos of trauma, the third dialogue cycle represents the failure of that endeavor. The disintegration of the third dialogue cycle reflects a collapse not only of effective dialogue, but of Job's social relationships. There is nothing left for Job and the friends to say to each other.

---

[7]Kathleen O'Connor, *Lamentations and the Tears of the World* (Maryknoll, NY: Orbis, 2002), 11. The exception to this format is the final poem, which does not follow the acrostic structure of the previous chapters.
[8]Seow, *Job 1–21*, 30.

Once this third dialogue cycle ends, there is a bit of detour in the text. It is as if a group of friends is in the midst of a massive argument when a great song comes on the radio, and everyone stops fighting and starts singing along. This is the perplexing Job 28. What is this chapter doing here and what does it mean? It seems, for many, like a something that doesn't fit . . . like one random curly fry in a box of onion rings. Job 28 has been called an interlude, a hymn, and an intermezzo. There is no general consensus who is speaking, and the text isn't clear. Is it Job? Is it the narrator popping in for an update? The content of the chapter seems to be at odds with what Job was saying in Job 27 and what he will say in Job 29. But if it isn't Job saying these words, who is it?

A trauma-informed reading approach cannot answer all of these questions, but it does propose that perhaps what we observe in Job 28 is a narrative pause of sorts. Job has been wrestling with the collapse of his fundamental beliefs and that is exhausting work. The odd nature of Job 28 may point to a need for a survivor to take a break from these big questions and rest for a moment. Have you ever had a dilemma that was so difficult or so emotionally draining that you just needed to set it aside for a little bit and watch a few episodes of your favorite sitcom? What may seem to be out of place or disconnected in Job 28 may be a sign of the depth of confusion Job has been going through. The seeming contradictions between this chapter and the surrounding chapters may also be a sign of the fragmentary and often contradictory nature of trauma, something we will explore more fully in a following section.

One final note on this third dialogue cycle. The literary disintegration of the third cycle reflects the breakdown in Job's relationships with the three friends, but it also mirrors the breakdown of Job's cognitive schemas. The dialogue format that had been established, the format expected by readers, is demolished without explanation. Not unlike Job's world. Without warning or explanation, Job's life is upended. His entire worldview and his understanding of God has been shattered . . . disintegrated in an instant. As Janoff-Bulman writes,

"The essence of trauma is the abrupt disintegration of one's inner world."[9] Job's most deeply held assumptions about the world have been shattered. As the third dialogue cycle reverts to disorganized chaos, we are reminded that Job's world is also still in chaos. As survivors and comforters, an awareness of the deep disintegration trauma causes will help us be aware of the larger issues that may be lurking beneath the surface. What looks like a messy divorce may be resting on top of a total collapse of someone's worldview. What looks like a hospital visit may in fact be a visit to someone who no longer knows how they fit into the world. Sitting with a parent who has lost a child may be sitting with someone who has lost their understanding of who God is.

DO WE HAVE TO TALK ABOUT THIS AGAIN?

When I was in labor with my son, I almost didn't make it to the hospital in time. Speed limits were broken, pain killers were not administered, curse words were said, and less than thirty minutes after arriving at the hospital our son was born. It was a terrifying and painful (quite literally) ordeal. I have told the story so many times that my kids know it by heart. Eighteen years later, I can laugh about it, but two days after my son's birth I did not find it funny at all. There is something in the act of repetition that helps us process, share, and understand our experiences.

This is especially true in the case of trauma. One of the often-observed characteristics of trauma processing is repetition. There are two elements of repetition that are important for us to understand. First, trauma survivors may return again and again to the memory of the traumatic experience. Second, survivors may talk about the experience over and over. Both of these types of repetition have an important purpose in trauma healing and resolution. Repetition, in its many forms, is a way for the mind to attempt to understand an event. If we return to the file cabinet metaphor, repetition is like continually picking up that paper we couldn't file, looking at it, and trying to figure out what to do with it. It

---

[9]Janoff-Bulman, *Shattered Assumptions*, 63.

is still sitting there on our desk, an outstanding item that needs to be filed, so we keep going back to it, re-examining it, trying to figure out a way to make it make sense. When it doesn't, we set it back on the desk and do something else, but eventually it will catch our eye again and we will return to it to see if this time we can figure it out and finally put it away.

Trauma expert Diane Langberg notes this prevalence of repetition in trauma survivors: "When people have been traumatized, they repeat things over and over, trying to grasp what cannot be understood and trying to carry what is unbearable."[10] Looking at the book of Job, Job returns again and again to his suffering. It is terrain Job cannot leave because he cannot yet understand it. Readers have the privilege of the prologue, Job does not. Readers understand what caused his losses, though the question of why is still a sticky one, but Job does not. And so, readers must journey with Job as he returns again and again to the site of his trauma, attempting in each return to understand what has befallen him. Job's suffering cannot be easily explained. It is like a piece of art that is so complex that each time you see it, you find something new. The trauma a survivor has experienced is so great, that it requires multiple visits to understand it.

Looking at the first type of repetition, returning to the memory of the traumatic event, these return trips may happen in flashbacks, nightmares, and intrusive thoughts. While a survivor may choose to remember the event and try to understand it, many times this type of repetition is not necessarily voluntary. Flashbacks and unwanted thoughts that pop up are beyond the survivor's control. They are reactions that are triggered by something else and take the survivor back, in some degree, to the traumatic event. The brain's survival instinct gets triggered and sets the emergency alarm system off to protect the survivor from further harm. It is an involuntary survival response. It brings the traumatic event back to the forefront of the survivor's mind and even though it may be overwhelming

---

[10]Diane Langberg, *Suffering and the Heart of God: How Trauma Destroys and Christ Restores* (Greensboro, NC: New Growth Press, 2015), 70.

and frightening to the survivor, it may also be an attempt by the mind to re-examine the traumatic event to try to better understand it and file it away. This can be alarming to the survivor's support community, but it may be a necessary part of the survivor's healing process. So, as comforters, our instinct to say, "Try not to think about that" or "Let it go" or "Stop dwelling on it" may be counterproductive. It might be exactly what the survivor needs to think about because the mind needs multiple returns to the event to understand the trauma. These intrusive memories that lead a survivor to re-experience or relive the trauma may be part of a complex process of cognitive reconstruction.[11]

One of the places we may be able to see an example of this type of repetition in the book is found in Job 29. After three lengthy dialogue cycles and going round and round with his friends for almost thirty chapters, Job's thoughts take him right back where he started.

Job again took up his discourse and said:
"O that I were as in the months of old,
    as in the days when God watched over me,
when his lamp shone over my head,
    and by his light I walked through darkness,
when I was in my prime,
    when the friendship of God was upon my tent,
when the Almighty was still with me,
    when my children were around me,
when my steps were washed with milk
    and the rock poured out for me streams of oil!
When I went out to the gate of the city,
    when I took my seat in the square,
the young men saw me and withdrew,
    and the aged rose up and stood;
the nobles refrained from talking
    and laid their hands on their mouths;

---

[11]Janoff-Bulman, *Shattered Assumptions*, 106.

the voices of princes were hushed,
and their tongues stuck to the roofs of their mouths." (Job 29:1-10)

Job goes back to his life before the losses and afflictions beset him. He notes first his previous relationship with YHWH. He yearns for a relationship that, to him, seems lost. He mentions his children and his former status in the community. The contrast between his previous sitting in the city gate as a respected man in the community and his current sitting in the ash heap is striking. This passage closes with a telling contrast between the nobles who once kept silent in his presence and the friends who have spent the past several chapters arguing with him, accusing him of wrongdoing, and insulting him. Job is without community comfort or support and without trusted listeners to hear his story, and so he returns again to the open file of the trauma. Job relives the traumatic events that brought him to the ash heap. It may be that within these types of repetitions, the trauma survivor attempts over and over to understand or make meaning of the events. As a survivor's support system, we need to be prepared for this type of repetition so we can be a support and not a hinderance to the healing process.

The second type of repetition is a trauma survivor needing to talk about their experience over and over again. It is normal and expected that survivors may need to talk about the trauma multiple times. Remember, trauma is a chaotic and disorganized event. It is stored not as an ordinary narrative memory, but as fragments. A survivor may not immediately be able to recall the totality of the event. They may only have pieces and fragments that need to be stitched together. Each time they tell the story they may be able to recover more of the details, or they may notice something new about it. There may be shifts and alterations in their telling. It is important for a trusted listener to be aware of this possibility. Instead of pouncing on a change in detail as evidence that the event did not happen or as an indication that the survivor is lying or not remembering things correctly and is therefore untrustworthy, these alterations and additions may be indicative of the severity of the trauma and the step-by-step process of accessing the fragmented memories of the event. We need to allow room for the development of the survivor's story. Expecting, or demanding, a full and complete tale of a traumatic event on the first telling is unreasonable and unsafe.

Scholar David Garber, in his work on trauma literature, has noted that because of the nature of trauma itself, trauma literature is often repetitive.[12] Thus, the text itself can become a literary representation of the repetitious nature of a traumatic experience. This is apparent in the book of Job as he and his friends debate and discuss. Even the cyclic nature of the dialogue cycles reflects the characteristic repetition of trauma. There is a performative aspect to the text that envelops readers in the cyclic nature of Job's trauma. Job cannot express his confusion and chaos once and be done. Instead, he has to return again and again, trying, in each visit, to understand that which cannot be understood. Readers, even knowing the cause of Job's suffering, are brought on a winding, round and round textual journey as Job remains stuck in the wreckage of his shattered life. "For trauma survivors, it is as if the mind becomes stuck in a playback loop. The mind keeps going over the scene of violence, again and again, often unconsciously, in an attempt to process it, but unable to do so. The mind's meaning-making structures have collapsed, so it simply repeats and recycles."[13] Sometimes we have to say something over and over before it feels real. This happens with triumphs as well as tragedies. When I won my first book award, it didn't feel real. The more I shared it, the more I heard other people say it, the more real it became until, finally, one day it sunk it. With things as powerful as grief, loss, and suffering, sometimes we have to talk about it, we have to say it over and over until it becomes something truly real that we can understand and accept. The need to talk about the trauma

---

[12]Garber, "I Went in Bitterness," 249.
[13]Serene Jones, *Trauma and Grace: Theology in a Ruptured World* (Louisville, KY: Westminster John Knox, 2019), 29.

multiple times is not a sign of unforgiveness, attention seeking, or an unwillingness to let it go, it is a sign of an ongoing healing process.

As comforters, we must be prepared for the repetitive nature of trauma. We may have to listen to the same story multiple times. We may have to tell a survivor the same thing over and over again. We will need to be sensitive to the fragmentary nature of the survivor's memories and the laborious effort it takes to stitch all those disjointed memories into something cohesive. This requires patience and a willingness to invest time and energy into being a trusted listener. It is no easy feat to sit down and read through the book of Job. In fact, before I wrote my dissertation on it, it was one of my least favorites books of the Bible. I found it repetitive and boring. Yes, Job, you're miserable and mad, we get it. Yes, friends, you think he needs to repent and move on, we get it. Can we skip ahead to God showing up in the whirlwind and giving everyone a what for? The book of Job reflects in words what the experience of trauma can feel like. It can feel repetitive and exhausting. But that is because trauma *is* repetitive and exhausting. To be invited into someone's pain is an honor not a burden. But too often we get it twisted. We think our job is to pick a survivor up from the ashes, dust them off, and send them right back into the world so everyone, including us, can move on. The reality of sitting in the ashes until the survivor is ready to stand on their own can be overwhelming and scary, but that is what we are called to do.

What Do I Believe?

One of the most disorienting things about trauma is the way our most deeply held beliefs may suddenly seem shaky. A rock that hits the side of our house is a problem. It may cause a dent that we need to fix or knock a shingle loose. It's a nuisance, but it can wait. But a rock that crashes through the window and exposes our home to danger . . . that is an emergency. We are vulnerable to the wind and rain, our home is open to the elements, broken glass litters the floor and cuts our feet. Burglars and birds can enter; we are no longer safe or protected. When we suffer trauma, we may no longer feel safe in the world. Our hope for the future may seem misplaced. Our view of God may suddenly seem wrong. Our trust in other people may be broken. The collapse of our cognitive schemas, those beliefs that color and affect how we experience and understand the world, leaves us adrift in a world that is suddenly dangerous, confusing, and chaotic. Trauma forces us to confront our beliefs and sometimes discard them. When what we thought we knew and understood about the world, God, and our place in creation is shaken, we have to rebuild those beliefs into something more resilient. We have to rebuild a window that can withstand the trauma we have endured. We see this confrontation with failed beliefs develop in the book of Job as he wrestles with what he believes and what he has found to no longer be true. We can trace the development of Job's failed schemas and his attempts at building new schemas, something called schematic testing, in the progress of the dialogue. We will explore the issue of finding meaning in trauma in a later chapter, but for now it is important that we recognize the role of schematic testing in trauma processing as it is something that we may encounter as both survivors and comforters.

In the dialogue cycles we see Job working through the cognitive dissonance that has followed the traumatic events of Job 1–2. While Job's friends remain entrenched in their retributive worldview and maintain staunch fidelity to their initial propositions, Job has no such loyalty as he tries on different explanatory schemas throughout the dialogue. Job's initial perspective in Job 3 evolves and shifts throughout the dialogue leading up to his climatic declaration of innocence before God in Job 31. As the dialogue progresses, Job tries on different ideas in an attempt to understand and explain his situation. His previous worldview and understanding of God (the Retribution Principle) have failed him, so he is trying to find another explanation. It's not unlike the unfortunate moment when we try on our favorite jeans and discover they no longer fit. Off to the store we go to try on pair after pair to find a new style and new size that will fit our new body-type reality.

Let's look at a few examples of how Job's perspective changes as he begins to try on different explanatory schemas searching for the right fit. In Job's first speech in Job 3, he is focused on his misery as he wishes he had never been born.

> Let the day perish in which I was born,
>> and the night that said,
>> "A male is conceived."
> Let that day be darkness!
>> May God above not seek it
>> or light shine on it.
> Let gloom and deep darkness claim it.
>> Let clouds settle upon it;
>> let the blackness of the day terrify it.
> That night—let thick darkness seize it!
>> let it not rejoice among the days of the year;
>> let it not come into the number of the months.
> Yes, let that night be barren;
>> let no joyful cry be heard in it. (Job 3:3-7)

Job's initial words are not to accuse God. Instead, his focus is on himself and his suffering. He wishes he had never been born. He wants his suffering to end. Yet, by the end of the third dialogue cycle in Job 27, his focus has shifted to YHWH's role in his suffering and his own steadfast commitment to his righteousness.

> As God lives, who has taken away my right,
>> and the Almighty, who has made my soul bitter,
> as long as my breath is in me
>> and the spirit of God is in my nostrils,
> my lips will not speak falsehood,
>> and my tongue will not utter deceit.
> Far be it from me to say that you are right;
>> until I die I will not put away my integrity from me.
> I hold fast my righteousness and will not let it go;
>> my heart will not reproach me as long as I live. (Job 27:2-6)

And by Job 31, he has moved to a formal legal defense with his oath of innocence.

> If I have made gold my trust
>   or called fine gold my confidence,
> if I have rejoiced because my wealth was great
>   or because my hand had gotten much,
> if I have looked at the sun when it shone
>   or the moon moving in splendor,
> and my heart has been secretly enticed,
>   and my mouth has kissed my hand,
> this also would be an iniquity to be punished by the judges,
>   for I should have been false to God above. (Job 31:24-28)

As Job talks, his perspective changes. Newsom argues that it is the form of dialogue that gives Job the space he needs to develop new imaginative possibilities that were not present, nor even conceivable, in the beginning of the dialogue cycles.[14] In other words, Job couldn't start out in Job 3 blaming God and crafting a lengthy legal defense. He gets there slowly, step by step, as he thinks through and talks through his experience. It is the process of dialogue that provides the means for Job to engage in ongoing schema testing.

Looking at the three dialogue cycles between Job and the friends, there is a clear development in Job's argumentation. Job's friends remain relatively static in their arguments that Job is to blame, and he needs to repent, though their words become more forceful and accusatory the more they talk. Job's arguments, however, shift and develop. Though the friends grow more vitriolic and aggressive in their arguments, overall, they end up where they started. They haven't budged one theological inch. They demonstrate cognitive conservatism and resistance to change. They know what they know and no evidence to the contrary will make them change their minds. For

---

[14]Carol Newsom, "The Book of Job as Polyphonic Text," *Journal for the Study of the Old Testament* 26, no. 3 (March 2002): 99.

example, the friends' call for Job to repent in order to end his suffering runs throughout the text and remains unchanged:

> As for me, I would seek God,
>> and to God I would commit my cause. (Job 5:8, Eliphaz)

> If you will seek God
>> and make supplication to the Almighty,
> if you are pure and upright,
>> surely then he will rouse himself for you
>> and restore to you your rightful place. (Job 8:5-6, Bildad)

> If you direct your heart rightly,
>> you will stretch out your hands toward him.
> If iniquity is in your hand, put it far away,
>> and do not let wickedness reside in your tents.
> Surely then you will lift up your face without blemish;
>> you will be secure and will not fear.
> You will forget your misery;
>> you will remember it as waters that have passed away.
> And your life will be brighter than the noonday;
>> its darkness will be like the morning.
> And you will have confidence because there is hope;
>> you will be protected and take your rest in safety.
> You will lie down, and no one will make you afraid;
>> many will entreat your favor. (Job 11:13-19, Zophar)

> Agree with God, and be at peace;
>> in this way good will come to you.
> Receive instruction from his mouth,
>> and lay up his words in your heart.
> If you return to the Almighty, you will be restored,
>> if you remove unrighteousness from your tents,
> if you treat gold like dust
>> and gold of Ophir like the stones of the torrent bed,
> and if the Almighty is your gold
>> and your precious silver,

then you will delight yourself in the Almighty
and lift up your face to God. (Job 22:21-26, Eliphaz)

Similarly, they refuse to change their commitment to their understanding of the doctrine of retribution. Even when face-to-face with
Job's suffering and protestations of innocence, they are incapable of
considering that their worldview, and thus their understanding of
Job's situation, is incorrect.

Think now, who that was innocent ever perished?
Or where were the upright cut off?
As I have seen, those who plow iniquity
and sow trouble reap the same. (Job 4:7-8, Eliphaz)

Surely the light of the wicked is put out,
and the flame of their fire does not shine.
The light is dark in their tent,
and the lamp above them is put out.
Their strong steps are shortened,
and their own schemes throw them down. (Job 18:5-7, Bildad)

For they [the wicked] knew no quiet in their bellies;
in their greed they let nothing escape.
There was nothing left after they had eaten;
therefore their prosperity will not endure.
In full sufficiency they will be in distress;
all the force of misery will come upon them.
To fill their belly to the full,
God will send his fierce anger into them
and rain it upon them as their food. (Job 20:20-23, Zophar)

The friends' inability, or unwillingness, to imagine a different
worldview or to recognize that their long-held schema may be incorrect, makes them incapable of engaging in the same type of cognitive adaptability as Job. Webb writes, "The debates represent
complex efforts in schema testing, as each speaker presents elements

of his conceptions of God and of universal justice."[15] While the friends remain adamantly devoted to their perspective, Job tries out different schemas in his arguments to see if any of them can adequately explain his situation.

In some places there is noticeable tension in Job's different explanatory schemas. This is important for comforters and trusted listeners because it shows that there are times when trauma survivors may be engaged in what seem like obvious contradictions. This takes us back to the fundamentals of traumatic memories as disjointed and disconnected. There is an inherent fragmentation of the experience because in the moment, it triggered the survivor's survival response. Energy and mental resources were shifted away from memory and shifted to ensuring survival, so the event was not processed like narrative memories. Instead, the memory of the event exists in fragments of experience, disjointed memories and sensations that must be put back together. Within these fragments, different perceptions and experiences of the event exist simultaneously and, at times, in contradiction. If we use our jigsaw puzzle metaphor here, a blue puzzle piece could be a piece of the sky, or it could be a piece of the ocean. Until we fit it into place, we can look at it and see both sea and sky at the same time. Obviously, the puzzle piece can't actually be two different things that contradict each other, but until we categorize it, we can think of it as both at the same time. The lack of narrative cohesion of a traumatic experience leaves it in pieces, like the shattered window glass on the floor. The disjointed nature of these memories can result in contradictions. We can see this in the book of Job, for example, in the way Job describes God:

> O that you would hide me in Sheol,
>> that you would conceal me until your wrath is past,
>> that you would appoint me a set time and remember me! (Job 14:13)

---

[15]Webb, "The Book of Job," 164.

For Job, God is his tormentor and enemy, and at the same time, God is also the One who will vindicate Job and restore him. In this verse, God is both the One who will hide Job to protect him and the One who inflicts wrath. Both images are true for Job at the same time. Job's understanding of God is splintered. For Job, God is both cruel and unfair, but also merciful and just.[16] Job is able to hold these contrasting images of God simultaneously because, for him, both are true. This is the fragmentary nature of trauma. Contrasting ideas can be held in tension because each fragment exists in its own nonlinear space and thus the opposing ideas can exist for the survivor at the same time. What doesn't make sense for comforters and those trying to support a trauma survivor does make sense to the survivor. These contradictory ideas are like the jigsaw puzzle piece that can be both sky and sea because it hasn't been put in place yet. As survivors and comforters, we must be willing to allow these contradictions to co-exist in the healing process until all the pieces are finally put in place.

We see in Job's struggles to understand his circumstances that trauma processing is neither linear nor logical. Webb writes, "It is not the case that persons generally proceed in rational, orderly, sequential trajectories from the world-view shattering experience of trauma to emotional and cognitive resolution."[17] As survivors, it can be easy to get discouraged in the healing process when it feels like we are taking two steps forward and one step back, but we need to remember that the journey to healing from trauma will not be neat and orderly with checkpoints to be crossed off at certain points. As comforters, we need to remember that choosing to come alongside a trauma survivor is not a short jaunt, it is a cross-country road trip with switchbacks and detours along the way. We cannot expect a quick trip that follows the map perfectly. We need to be prepared for the repetition, the

---

[16]Michael V. Fox, "The Meanings of the Book of Job," *Journal of Biblical Literature* 137, no. 1 (2018): 10.

[17]Webb, "The Book of Job," 168.

circling back, the contradictions, and the crisis of belief. Recognizing the messiness and chaos of processing traumatic experiences allows for trauma survivors' stories to be similarly messy and at times chaotic.

LESSONS LEARNED

- The dialogue cycles in the book of Job not only reflect the important role of talking and sharing in the process of trauma healing, but they also reflect the desire to impose order or organization on a chaotic and disorganized experience.

- Repetition plays an important role in trauma healing. Survivors may need to talk about their experience multiple times in the healing journey.

- Because trauma is often remembered in fragments and pieces, sharing the story of a trauma-inducing event may not start out with a clear beginning, middle, and an end.

REFLECTION QUESTIONS

- Who is the first person you go to when you have something you want to talk about, whether good or bad? What makes that person a trusted listener for you?

- What is an experience you have been through where your perspective changed after you spoke with a trusted friend or comforter?

- Does understanding more about trauma change how you view Job's words throughout the dialogue cycles?

FIVE

WHEN WORDS FAIL

ABOUT NINE YEARS AGO, I suffered second degree burns on my legs. The burn on my right leg was significantly worse and required daily debriding treatment to prevent infection. It was, without a doubt, the worst pain I have ever experienced (and, as I mentioned in the previous chapter, I have been through natural childbirth). The pain was absolutely breathtaking. Pain killers didn't help much because the nerves in my leg were traumatized by the burn and wouldn't stop firing. It was two weeks of never-ending, all-consuming pain. It was the only thing I could think about. I couldn't walk. I couldn't sleep. It was pain like I had never experienced before, and I didn't have the words to describe it accurately. When the doctor would ask "on a scale of one to ten, how's your pain level?" I would stare at her, because even ten wasn't enough.

That's what trauma does to us. It smashes through our normal frame of reference and catapults us into a realm we've never seen before. Just like the burn on my leg took me to a level of pain that I didn't know existed, trauma takes us to a place we've never been. It's a whole new world, but it's a dark and terrifying world filled with creatures we can't name. It is a world that we can't explain. There are literally no words for these new experiences. It would be like abducting a first-century Roman and dropping them in New York City for a day and then taking them back to their first-century village and asking them to describe what they had seen. They simply wouldn't have the words to describe skyscrapers, airplanes, cars, and hot dogs. How do you describe something that you have never seen before, something that exists in a totally different world? And how do you describe it in a way that the people around you, who didn't see the helicopters, buses, and neon billboards, would understand?

This failure of language is one of the things that makes it so difficult to share our trauma. We are suddenly dropped into a new world and then asked to describe it. If trauma shatters the window through which we perceived the world, then our normal categories of understanding have been shattered too. Trauma overwhelms our existing explanatory schemas. It doesn't fit into any of our mental files, so it lingers as an unresolved and fragmentary experience. We can't categorize it or file it away because it's a mess of disorganized snippets of information. It's like getting a big box of unassembled furniture pieces with no instructions. Is it a desk? Is it a bookcase? Is it a wardrobe that leads to Narnia? We can't describe or explain that which we don't understand.[1] And trauma is incomprehensible . . . that's one of the things that makes it trauma.

Trauma resists quick and easy description because there are no words that can accurately describe an experience that even the survivor does not yet fully understand. As Rambo writes, "language falters in the abyss; it fractures at the site of trauma."[2] Language fails survivors not because of any deficiency or fault by the survivor. It's not because we don't know enough words or have trouble expressing ourselves. It is not the survivor who fails, but language itself that fails.[3] When we use

---

[1]Elizabeth Boase, "'Whispered in the Sound of Silence': Traumatising the Book of Jonah," *The Bible and Critical Theory* 12, no. 1 (2016): 11.

[2]Shelly Rambo, *Spirit and Trauma: A Theology of Remaining* (Louisville, KY: Westminster John Knox, 2010), 164.

[3]David Janzen, "Claimed and Unclaimed Experience: Problematic Readings of Trauma in the Hebrew Bible," *Biblical Interpretation* 27, no. 2 (2019): 176.

language, the words act as symbols that point to concepts. The word *building* is not an actual building, but it points us to the concept of a building. You say *building* and I understand, to some extent, what you mean. It is a category we both understand and can utilize for effective communication. Language is an agreed-on map that we all follow. We all agree that in English *dog* means a four-legged creature descended from wolves that is often a house pet. But in Hebrew "dog" sounds a lot like *dag*, the word for fish. Hebrew uses a different agreed-on map, so even though the words sound similar, they actually mean very different things. Trauma, by its nature, exceeds ordinary concepts, it breaks accepted categories, it goes beyond comprehension. There are literally no words available that can accurately describe a previously unknown and undefined experience, an experience that the survivor and their trusted comforter do not share.

When people experience trauma, they often experience "speechless terror."[4] Remember, trauma is a physiological response designed to ensure survival. Survival becomes the body's primary objective. This physiological response not only impacts the way the experience is stored as a memory, but it also inhibits the way we talk about it. Normal memory processes are altered as the mind and body focus on survival. It's an emergency response where the priority is keeping the patient alive, and we worry about the niceties later. Because the brain and body are in survival mode, the experience itself cannot be organized in a neat, narrative format. The energy and resources needed for that kind of memory processing are being diverted to other areas of the brain to make sure we stay alive. With these limited memory resources, the experience is stored instead in fragments and pieces. These pieces don't go in the filing cabinet, instead they remain on the desk and may pop up unexpectedly.[5] In order to get all of the fragments back into

---

[4]Bessel van der Kolk and Onno van der Hart, "The Intrusive Past: The Flexibility of Memory and the Engraving of Trauma," in *Trauma: Explorations in Memory*, ed. Cathy Caruth (Baltimore, MD: Johns Hopkins University Press, 1995), 172.

[5]Van der Kolk and van der Hart, "The Intrusive Past," 172.

one coherent narrative that can then be filed away in a healthy manner, the trauma survivor needs to be able to express what has happened, but the insufficiency of language to explain the trauma means they cannot.[6] To communicate the experience, the survivor must rely on language, but that language has proven to be inadequate. This contradiction lies at the heart of the incommunicability of trauma.

As comforters, we need to be aware of this failure of language. When we come alongside someone who has experienced trauma, we may face language barriers. Not because we speak different cultural languages, though that may be in some cases, but because there is a barrier between what the survivor has experienced and what they can communicate. Additionally, there is a barrier between what the survivor has experienced and what we, as witnesses and friends, have experienced. Notice, in the book of Job, the problems between Job and his friends didn't start until words got involved. For language to be effective, both speaker and listener must be drawing from the same linguistic map.[7] This applies most obviously to cultural languages like English, Spanish, and Korean. Having traveled a great deal in my life I have been face-to-face with language barriers that require creativity (and charades) to get past. However, this linguistic map also applies to the gulf between a survivor's experience and a witness's lack of that experience. We may both be speaking English, but we no longer share the same reference space.

I can point to my children here as an example. Rizz. Vibe. Bet. Excuse me? I'm a well-educated, articulate woman, and I know we're all speaking English but there is a linguistic gulf between us. We are no longer operating within the same language map. The good news is they can teach me, and I can learn (and then use this knowledge to be a cool mom). This same concept applies to trauma. The experience a survivor has walked through has changed their reference space. What they

---

[6]Serene Jones, *Trauma and Grace: Theology in a Ruptured World* (Louisville, KY: Westminster John Knox, 2019), 17.
[7]Lance Hawley, *Metaphor Competition in the Book of Job* (Göttingen: Vandenhoeck & Ruprecht, 2018), 15.

conceive of when they hear words like *pain, loss, helplessness, control*, and the emotional and physical reactions they feel may not be even remotely close to what the trusted listener is thinking. Their previously shared space of language has been destroyed by trauma.[8] The survivor and the witness are, in many ways, no longer speaking the same language, or at least they have different dialects now. "Trauma by nature drives us to the edge of comprehension, cutting us off from language based on common experience or an imaginable past."[9] This crisis of language experienced by the survivor becomes a crisis of relationality as a literal language barrier is erected around the survivor's experience of trauma. This in turn, reinforces the social separateness many trauma survivors feel. The social connection created by shared language has been damaged and the miscommunications that result can increase the survivor's sense of isolation and loneliness. The very words that should draw us together instead drive a wedge between us.

When we sit with a trauma survivor in silence, holding them when they cry or praying from afar because we heard of their situation from others, that silence allows us to make assumptions, and those assumptions will go unchallenged . . . until the survivor starts to speak. We may, like Job's friends, get entrenched in those assumptions, how we think the survivor should be feeling, what we think they should do, how we think we would react. Then words get involved. When the survivor is ready to speak, we must be ready to listen. The obstacle that arises at this moment though is that, for a trauma survivor, words are both necessary and elusive. As those supporting and caring for a survivor, we have to be prepared for this language barrier and recognize that it is a normal and expected part of a trauma response. It is not a failure by the survivor, it is a failure of language itself.

---

[8] Ruth Poser, "No Words: The Book of Ezekiel as Trauma Literature and a Response to Exile," in *Bible Through the Lens of Trauma*, ed. Elizabeth Boase and Christopher Frechette (Atlanta: SBL Press, 2016), 34.
[9] Van der Kolk, *The Body Keeps the Score*, 43.

The Poetry of Trauma

When we understand the physiology of a trauma response and its impact on language, we may begin to understand why so much of the text of the book of Job is in the form of poetry. It is difficult to put trauma into a straightforward narrative because the memories of the traumatic experience exist in a fragmented, nonnarrative state. They are a jumble of images, feelings, and jagged pieces of the puzzle that are scattered around the remains of our shattered window. As survivors, we may struggle to describe the experience because no words seem to fit.[10] A new type of language is needed.[11] Now, this is not to suggest that trauma survivors need to learn a new cultural language or that they need to take up interpretive dance. What we are recognizing here is the insufficiency of the survivor's existing language *references* to express, describe, and find meaning in the traumatic experience. What the survivor needs is flexibility in language. We may see this in metaphor, narrative retelling, and, as we see in the book of Job, poetry. Now, before we go tell the trauma survivors to whom we minister to start writing poetry (which isn't necessarily a bad idea), let's look at what the book of Job shows us about the relationship between language, poetry, and trauma and then seek to apply this information to our ministerial contexts.

What makes poetry useful in expressing trauma? June Frances Dickie notes the value of poetry in connection with a survivor's attempts to express their trauma: "Poetry has a particular value at times of disorientation."[12] She observes four particular aspects of poetry that make it well suited to trauma expression: (1) poetry is nonlinear and does not require narrative coherence; (2) poetry is image based; (3) the form and rhythm of poetry and intentional interruptions in each create tension and space for transformation; and (4) the metonymic

---

[10]Kathleen O'Connor, *Jeremiah: Pain and Promise* (Minneapolis: Fortress Press, 2012), 24.

[11]Anne Whitehead, *Trauma Fiction* (Edinburgh: University of Edinburgh Press, 2004), 6.

[12]June Frances Dickie, "Lament as a Contributor to the Healing of Trauma: An Application of Poetry in the Form of Biblical Lament," *Pastoral Psychology* 68, no. 2 (April 2019): 148.

quality of poetry allows one word to represent the entirety of an experience.[13] Let's look at those four elements. First, poetry is nonlinear. That is part of the beauty of poetry: it does not have to follow narrative conventions or timelines. Given what we have learned about how traumatic memories are stored as fragments without narrative format, this connection between poetry and trauma makes sense. Second, poetry is image based. Again, this shows a connection to the way in which the fragments of a traumatic experience are often remembered as images or sensory snippets. Third, the form of poetry has space for transformation. The gaps in poetry are spaces where imagination and creative transformation can happen. The flexibility of the form allows for transformative space. Just as we saw in Job's silence, it is sometimes within the gaps that change occurs. Finally, the metonymic quality of poetry allows for one word to point to the totality of an experience without having to define it. For example, if we see a friend's new car we may say, "Nice new wheels." We don't mean only the wheels are new, but we are using "wheels" to point to the entire new car. This pointing element of poetry can allow survivors to begin to access and describe the trauma before they have all the words needed to go into detail. One word can stand for everything that remains indescribable.

By the end of Job 2, Job is utterly overwhelmed by his losses and is reduced to silence. When he speaks again in Job 3 it is in poetry. O'Connor insightfully notes of this transition that "to cross from the prose prologue into the poetry in the book is to move into an altered world."[14] It is not just a slip from one genre to another, instead, the change from prose to poetry marks a crossing into a new world. Job's most fundamental beliefs have been shattered. Language has failed him, but silence has failed him as well. He opens his mouth to speak, but what pours forth is not the orderly, linear words of prose, instead we encounter the nonlinear, metaphorical words of poetry. Job

---

[13]Dickie, "Lament as a Contributor," 148.
[14]Kathleen O'Connor, *Job* (Collegeville, MN: Liturgical Press, 2012), 15.

abandons the narrative format of the first two chapters and embarks on a poetic expression of his pain. He relies on the nonlinear, imagery-filled flexibility of poetry to give words to his trauma.

It is the imaginative space within poetry that gives Job the ability to start processing his trauma. As we have seen, he engages in schema testing as he tries to understand what has befallen him. He uses metaphors, sometimes shocking and challenging metaphors, to express what he is going through. The use of poetry also provides him with needed distance, a distance that allows Job to speak indirectly or euphemistically about his trauma. This distance functions as a protection against the threat of being overwhelmed for trauma survivors as they engage with traumatic memories.[15] When we are facing something awful, sometimes we need a bit of linguistic distance to give us some breathing room. We see this in language all the time, as, for example, when we say someone has "passed away" or "been called home" as opposed to using the word *died.* Or when we personally are struggling with something and frame it as "when a person battles addiction" as opposed to stating, "when I battle addiction." Similarly, we see Job often using metaphors to describe his losses, rather than explicitly stating them.

> For the arrows of the Almighty are in me;
>> my spirit drinks their poison;
>> the terrors of God are arrayed against me. (Job 6:4)

Job relies here on indirect, poetic speech to refer to his trauma. The metaphors of *arrows, poison,* and *terrors* stand in for the literal losses he has endured. Job is talking about his suffering, but in an indirect and metaphorical way. It is left to the prose narrator to describe the specifics of Job's losses: his livestock, his wealth, his children, and his health. In the poetic section, Job will use vivid and graphic language to symbolically describe his situation and his feelings, but he does not simply state,

---

[15]Christopher G. Frechette, "The Old Testament as Controlled Substance: How Insights from Trauma Studies Reveal Healing Capacities in Potentially Harmful Texts," *Interpretation* 69, no. 1 (January 2015): 28.

for example, "my children were killed." Instead, he uses poetry to testify to his suffering while maintaining distance from the specifics. It is the indirect nature of poetry that allows Job to engage repeatedly with his traumatic experience. As he returns again and again using new and different metaphors, he gets closer to resolution and healing.

So, what does this tell us as survivors and comforters about trauma and language? It shows us that sometimes indirect speech is a necessary part of trauma processing. There may be times when the trauma survivors we support cannot speak directly about the event. They may not be able to describe their situation or their feelings eloquently and completely. It may be that their mind is relying on poetic-type language to protect them from being overwhelmed and crushed by the memories of their experience. We may hear a survivor say something like "I feel like I'm trapped," or "I'm suffocating," or "everything is gone." These are powerful and emotional statements that may be pointing to specifics they can't currently name. Again, this is a normal trauma response. As trusted listeners it is not our job to push survivors to name and claim their experience before they are ready. We may need to travel the winding and twisting road with them until they can find the right words on their own. It may be a lengthy process, it may be frustrating at times, but the goal here is not a quick resolution, the goal is a healthy resolution. We may need to engage in just as much creativity as we listen to and try to understand the words they choose. Job's friends couldn't do that. They took Job's words personally and reacted defensively. Instead of receiving his words and engaging them with curiosity and humility, Job's friends attempted to instruct Job on his own experience. Can I say that one more time? Job's friends tried to instruct Job about his own experience. As trusted listeners we need to be students, not teachers. Our desire to help a survivor, lead them, and guide them out of their pain is admirable, but it cannot be forced or imposed. We cannot explain the survivor's trauma, we can only walk with them as they find meaning in their experience. We can offer our opinion. We can offer sound biblical teaching. We can encourage them to talk and process, but we need to have curiosity and compassion and be willing to learn about the survivor's experience, their feelings, their struggles, and their healing. The survivor is the expert on their experience, not us. If we see a survivor we care about struggling to put the pieces back together, our best option may be to refer them to a qualified trauma counselor and then walk with them through a process that is led by someone else.

TRAUMA IS LIKE . . .

When words fail, we often turn to metaphors and similes to try to get our point across. Figurative language isn't just window dressing in the way we communicate. Metaphors, similes, and other forms of figurative language serve an important function that goes beyond getting extra credit in a creative writing assignment. If we go back to our idea of a first-century Roman being dropped in Times Square and then having to tell his village about everything he saw, we can imagine the struggle he would have describing the strange sights and sounds. When trying to describe an airplane, he might say it was a gigantic bird without feathers that spewed smoke. Metaphors help bridge a gap in understanding. If we can't find the right words, we will find the closest words. We see this use of metaphor and figurative language play out in both the book of Job and in trauma processing.

Why is it important that we be aware of the role of metaphor in trauma? Telling the story of a traumatic experience is not a "just the facts, ma'am" type of situation. Trauma is a response to an event, or events, that overwhelms a survivor's existing cognitive framework. It shatters the window and crashes through their world. If we imagine a car accident or another sudden and unexpected event, we can understand how the memory of that event becomes jumbled and fragmented in our minds. Everything happens so fast that sometimes we can only catch snippets of the experience. We may not remember everything;

in fact, we may remember the smallest detail and forget something big. For example, when I remember the time the brakes in my car failed on the freeway in Washington, DC, I remember the sound of the alarm blaring in my car like some sci-fi self-destruct button and the feel of the brake pedal going all the way to the floor with no resistance. I remember looking at the brake lights of the car in front of me, and I remember the terror on my daughter's face. I remember the prayer I whispered when I was sure we were going to die. But I don't remember what the cars around me looked like. I don't remember what time of day it was. I don't even remember the name of the exit I managed to get to or the name of the commuter lot where I coasted until my car finally rolled to a stop. If you ask me to tell the story fifty times, I may goof up the location on the freeway or which part of DC we were in, but I can tell you the sights and sounds and emotions that I experienced in great detail. It is the fragmentary nature of those memories coupled with the physiological alarm system of a lingering trauma response that can make the telling of a traumatic event so difficult.

That is where metaphor comes in. Metaphors (and similes and other types of figurative language) function as pointers. They point us to something else, something we can't quite describe. Let's look at a metaphor from the book of Job as an example.

One wastes away like a rotten thing,
    like a garment that is moth-eaten. (Job 13:28)

This verse is particularly poignant for our discussion of trauma. It illustrates not only the beautiful artistry of the poetry in the book of Job, but it contains powerful emotional content. Job is comparing himself to wasting away like something rotting, like a garment that is being eaten by moths. Within the context of trauma, it is not simply a beautiful and evocative metaphor, it is a signpost pointing to something else. Job doesn't just come out and identify his emotions. "I am feeling overwhelmed by sadness, worn out by my pain, and eaten up with grief."

No, he uses a graphic and descriptive metaphor to point to the reality of his suffering through figurative language. Here is another example:

> He has torn me in his wrath and hated me;
>> he has gnashed his teeth at me;
>> my adversary sharpens his eyes against me.
> They have gaped at me with their mouths;
>> they have struck me insolently on the cheek;
>> they mass themselves together against me.
> God gives me up to the evil
>> and casts me into the hands of the wicked.
> I was at ease, and he broke me in two;
>> he seized me by the neck and dashed me to pieces;
>> he set me up as his target;
>> his archers surround me.
> He slashes open my kidneys and shows no mercy;
>> he pours out my gall on the ground. (Job 16:9-13)

In this section, Job is directing the blame for his circumstances at God. It is God who has gnashed his teeth at Job, God who has dashed Job to pieces, God who has slashed open his kidneys and shown Job no mercy. Again, the vividness and graphic detail of the language is pointing to the stunning pain Job is enduring. Have his kidneys actually been slashed open? No, but it is the only way Job can describe what he is feeling. He uses these shocking metaphors to try to describe the indescribable.

Given the failure of language to adequately express an experience of trauma, trauma theorists point to the important role of metaphor and visual imagery in trauma narratives.[16] As we see in the above examples

---

[16]See, for example, J. Anker, "Metaphors of Pain: The Use of Metaphors in Trauma Narrative with Reference to Fugitive Pieces," *Literator* 30, no. 2 (August 2009): 49-68; L. Juliana Claassens, *Writing and Reading to Survive: Biblical and Contemporary Trauma Narrative in Conversation* (Sheffield, UK: Sheffield Phoenix Press, 2020); Ronald Granofsky, *The Trauma Novel: Contemporary Symbolic Depictions of Collective Disaster* (New York: Peter Lang Inc., 1995); Margaret Wilkinson, "Undoing Trauma: Contemporary Neuroscience; A Jungian Clinical Perspective," *The Journal of Analytical Psychology* 48, no. 2 (April 2003): 235-53.

from the book of Job, what cannot be said directly can, perhaps, be said indirectly. Metaphors can be the bridge between what a survivor cannot literally describe and their need to tell the story. Wilkinson adds that metaphor may be particularly well-suited to trauma processing because of its "power to re-establish the integrated working together of the two hemispheres of the brain after trauma."[17] The physiological impact of trauma on the language center of the brain and the resulting failure of language may be overcome by the use of metaphor and symbolic language. This connection reminds us that trauma is not just an emotional response, but it has significant physiological effects as well.

How do metaphors and figurative language work in the context of trauma? If you will bear with me for a brief detour into the realm of metaphor theory, we'll see how this works in real-time in trauma processing. Metaphors function most basically as providing a means to see one thing in terms of another.[18] Metaphors are not simply symbols where the symbol stands in for something else. Rather, metaphors and similes highlight certain similarities between the metaphor being used (the source) and the thing being pointed to (the target). Metaphors thus act as pointers as one concept, the source, is used to point to another, the target. When we encounter something new, metaphors help us conceptualize it by drawing on concepts we already understand. For example, when my daughter was two, we visited my dad and stepmother. They had two dogs, a small, fluffy dog and a big boxer. Our daughter was familiar with our dog at home, who was small and yappy. When she met my dad's small dog she said "doggy?" When she met the big boxer she said "horsey!" She did not have a frame of reference for a big dog, so she drew on the closet reference she had . . . a horse. We corrected her and she learned that dogs can be both small and big. But her first attempt to categorize and understand this new

---

[17]Wilkinson, "Undoing Trauma," 248.
[18]Antal Borbely, "A Psychoanalytic Concept of Metaphor," *The International Journal of Psycho-Analysis* 79, no. 5 (1998), 923.

creature was to use something she was already familiar with. Metaphors thus allow for connecting, or mapping, one domain, the *source* domain, to another more abstract domain, the *target* domain, in a way that facilitates a better understanding of the target concept.[19] With trauma being an experience that falls outside of our established cognitive framework, it is especially important that we see the role metaphor can play in helping us create new categories.[20]

However, and here's where it gets tricky, being able to understand a metaphor and grasp what it is pointing to requires shared knowledge and shared basic beliefs between the speaker and hearer.[21] So here we can see one of the reasons why Job and his friends end up at odds with each other. Job's traumatic experience has shattered his fundamental assumptions and called his worldview into question. His friends however have maintained those assumptions. There is a fundamental disconnect between Job's new conceptual world and the old conceptual world of his friends. "Job's suffering presents a challenge to the shared source world of Job and his friends because it calls into question their value system and basic beliefs about matters such as the cause-and-effect nature of retribution."[22] Job's experience of suffering has removed him from the shared knowledge source of his friends and potentially creates an obstacle in metaphor mapping and comprehension. The disconnect leads to a battle of metaphors that neither side can fully comprehend. Job's experience has led him to reject the shared world he previously inhabited and the friends are unable to accept Job's new and developing views. What Job describes indirectly via metaphoric language as injustice, the friends describe as retribution.

This demonstrates again the need for us as comforters to be students of the survivor's experience. In our sitting with a trauma survivor and

---

[19]Hawley, *Metaphor Competition*, 46.
[20]Anker, "Metaphors of Pain," 56.
[21]Hawley, *Metaphor Competition*, 15.
[22]Hawley, *Metaphor Competition*, 15.

listening to their story, we have to make an intentional effort to understand *their* language and *their* source world. If we listen to their words from only our perspective, we may miss the very thing they are trying to communicate. What does it mean when the survivor says, "I feel like I've lost a leg"? The only person who can answer that question is the survivor. What are their metaphors pointing to? What is the specific correspondence they are drawing between "I feel empty" and the trauma response they are going through? Additionally, the language trauma survivors use may be filled with extremes. Just as Job used graphic and violent metaphors of his kidneys being slashed open and his skin being clothed with worms, trauma survivors may similarly use shocking and extreme language as they try to convey the pain that are enduring. Remember, language fails in trauma. This is not the fault of the survivor; it is a normal physiological response to an overwhelming event as the brain's trauma response shifts energy and focus to survival. It is expected and should not be judged as weakness or lack of ability. Just as trauma does violence to the survivor's life, it also does violence to language. The extremes of language are pushed to the limits, just as the extremes of cognitive processing are pushed beyond their limits by the trauma.[23] So when a survivor says "I hate her," or "I want him to suffer," we can recognize the turmoil behind those words and start looking for the targets those words point to . . . issues like justice, recompense, fear, and a lack of safety.

When we sit with a trauma survivor, we need not only compassion, care, and patience, we may also need to learn a new language. If the assumptions we made in the silence can be proven wrong, the understanding we have of the metaphors they use may also be wrong. When we come alongside someone who has endured the unimaginable, whose entire world has been rocked, whose sense of safety and security has been stripped away, this isn't the time to assume we know what's going on. Job's

---

[23]Poser, "No Words," 44.

friends came to comfort Job, but they ended up wounding him because they could not walk through Job's experience with him. They needed Job to conform to their worldview, a reaction that is all too common for trauma survivors and one we will explore a bit later on. When we see extremes in language that we don't understand, perhaps our best option is to ask questions. Instead of judging or correcting the metaphors the survivor chooses to use, dig into them. What do you mean by that? How does your life feel empty? Why do you feel broken? When you say you've lost everything, what do you mean? If we start with a belief that the survivor's trauma response is normal and did its job to ensure survival, then perhaps we will stop seeing their response as something to be fixed and forgotten and view it instead as something to be understood and honored.

LESSONS LEARNED

- Trauma has a physiological impact on the way we use language, so, as trauma survivors, it may be difficult for us to put our experience into words.

- When we can't find the right words, metaphors can help. Metaphors offer us a way to use one concept to point to another more difficult to explain concept.

- Shocking or graphic language, like the language Job uses, can be an indicator of deeper emotions that a survivor cannot yet articulate.

REFLECTION QUESTIONS

- Why does the Bible include the type of graphic language and metaphors we see in the book of Job?

- Many of the metaphors Job uses are shocking. What would you do if you heard someone in your church community speaking the way Job speaks?

- When you pray, do you feel free to say anything to God? Or are you careful in the words you choose? Why?

SIX

WHERE IS THE JUSTICE?

MANY TRAUMA SURVIVORS are still waiting for an apology. They wait and wait, but . . . nothing. The people who harmed them have moved on with their lives, utterly unconcerned with the destruction they left in their wake. It's painful. It's heartbreaking. It's not fair. And that's the ugly truth of wounding and trauma. It's *not* fair. So many times, the justice we desire, the justice we deserve, never comes. The apologies we are owed are never spoken. It becomes one more layer of solitude and suffering brought about by trauma, the silence of the unrepentant. It is the longing for justice we may never get; the yearning for an acknowledgment that will never be given. I wrote an Instagram post a few months ago that read simply, "Some people would rather lose you than face the pain they caused." The human instinct to hide from the pain we cause, to avoid the shame and responsibility, looms large over our broken world and allows the wreckage to fester. Imagine how much pain could be avoided with the words, "I'm sorry I hurt you." But the interaction between the wounded, the wounder, and the bystander is complex and multifaceted. It is an interaction that has been often misunderstood and turned against trauma survivors.

When the wounding involves issues of power, authority, and influence, especially in a church environment, it becomes even more destructive, both for the wounded and the wounding.

The longing many trauma survivors have for justice is a normal part of a trauma response. When we are wronged, we want that wrong to be made right. We see this in parks and playdates, in elementary schools and corporate boardrooms, the idea of fairness, the sense that justice should be prevail. And yet, many times when we are confronted with unfairness, injustice, and wounding there is no remedy in sight. This tension between justice and injustice dwells inside the trauma response for many survivors. One of the places we see this in the book of Job is in the legal metaphor that runs through the text.

In the last chapter, we discussed the function of metaphors in language to serve as pointers. We also saw how metaphors and figurative language are important in trauma processing. While there isn't space here to discuss all of the metaphors in the book of Job (there are many and they are fascinating), I do want to spend some time looking at the legal metaphor in the text and how it highlights certain aspects of a trauma response. There are three distinct correspondences between the legal metaphor in the book of Job and trauma processing that we will look at: justice, passive bystanders, and revenge fantasies. In discussing where and how these appear in the book of Job, we will see how they also appear in trauma responses and, perhaps most importantly, how we can apply this information to the life of the church.

THE LEGAL METAPHOR

Throughout the book of Job, there are numerous occurrences of legal terminology, forensic language, and courtroom images. It is a motif that develops and grows throughout the dialogue cycles and reaches a climax in Job's declaration of his innocence in Job 29–31. As Job wrestles with his losses, he repeatedly cries out for an audience with God. Convinced of his innocence of any sin that would warrant the type of punishment he has endured, Job expresses his desire to meet with God. One of the ways Job formulates this yearning is with the use of a legal metaphor. Newsom writes,

> Even if it is a chimerical hope, the notion of a trial organizes his [Job's] energy. The lawsuit metaphor appears in only a limited number of verses, yet it occupies an increasingly important place in Job's imagination . . . until it becomes the mode by which Job attempts to force a confrontation with God.[1]

The idea of a lawsuit first appears in Job 9.

> Indeed, I know that this is so,
>> but how can a mortal be just before God?
> If one wished to contend with him,
>> one could not answer him once in a thousand. (Job 9:2-3)

The Hebrew word *lariv*, translated here as "to contend," carries connotations of conflict and disputation, including legal disputation.[2] Job latches onto this idea of bringing YHWH to court and runs with it. A few verses later, Job further develops this lawsuit idea, even as he recognizes the difficulty in trying to bring God to court:

> How then can I answer him,
>> choosing my words with him?
> Though I am innocent, I cannot answer him;
>> I must appeal to my accuser for my right.
> If I summoned him and he answered me,
>> I do not believe that he would listen to my voice.
> For he crushes me with a tempest
>> and multiplies my wounds without cause;
> he will not let me get my breath
>> but fills me with bitterness.

---

[1] Carol Newsom, "The Book of Job," in *The New Interpreters Bible*, vol. 4 (Nashville: Abingdon Press, 1996), 363.

[2] David J. A. Clines, *Job 1–20* (Grand Rapids, MI: HarperCollins Christian, 1989), 227.

> If it is a contest of strength, he is the strong one!
> > If it is a matter of justice, who can summon him?
> Though I am innocent, my own mouth would condemn me;
> > though I am blameless, he would prove me perverse. (Job 9:14-20)

How can Job bring charges against God when God himself is the judge? This contradiction makes sense in light of what we have learned already about trauma, schema testing, and fragmentation. Job is trying out different possibilities and even though he recognizes the inconsistencies, he still holds these contradictory ideas simultaneously. That is the tension that comes with processing fragment and shards of trauma. Even in spite of the overwhelming odds against him, Job does not let go of the idea of a lawsuit, and he returns to it repeatedly throughout the text.

As the legal metaphor develops, Job's desire to be vindicated strengthens:

> Listen carefully to my words,
> > and let my declaration be in your ears.
> I have indeed prepared my case;
> > I know that I shall be vindicated. (Job 13:17-18)

Job asks for the list of charges of which he has been accused.

> How many are my iniquities and my sins?
> > Make me know my transgression and my sin. (Job 13:23)

This verse demonstrates that Job believes the afflictions he has suffered imply that he has already been found guilty.[3] And Job may not be far off in his reasoning. The connections between sin and suffering, and righteousness and reward inherent in the retributive theology of Job's friends would certainly seem to support the idea that Job's afflictions are evidence that he is being punished for sin. Job himself acknowledges this in Job 16:

---

[3]Michael Brennan Dick, "The Legal Metaphor in Job 31," *The Catholic Biblical Quarterly* 41, no. 1 (January 1979): 39.

And he [God] has shriveled me up,
>   which is a witness against me. (Job 16:8)

This idea that Job's losses and physical afflictions are evidence that testify against him is used by the friends to support their contention that Job is guilty of wrongdoing and that is why he is suffering. In fact, Eliphaz pulls no punches with Job. The friend that was so deferential and gentle at the start turns and accuses Job of a long list of sin and cruelty:

Is it for your piety that he reproves you
>   and enters into judgment with you?
Is not your wickedness great?
>   There is no end to your iniquities.
For you have exacted pledges from your family for no reason
>   and stripped the naked of their clothing.
You have given no water to the weary to drink,
>   and you have withheld bread from the hungry.
The powerful possess the land,
>   and the favored live in it.
You have sent widows away empty-handed,
>   and the arms of the orphans you have crushed.
Therefore snares are around you,
>   and sudden terror overwhelms you,
or darkness so that you cannot see;
>   a flood of water covers you. (Job 22:4-11)

Eliphaz, perhaps exasperated with Job's refusal to abandon his claims of innocence and integrity, accuses Job directly of several sins and argues these sins are why Job has been punished by God.

As the legal metaphor develops, Job comes to see himself as a man who has been wrongfully accused and punished. His search for vindication will eventually culminate in his oath of innocence in Job 31. Job's final speech in Job 29–31 is "a daring step in a final attempt to clear himself."[4] In Job 31, he offers an oath of innocence and a request for a legal hearing.[5]

> If I have walked with falsehood,
>> and my foot has hurried to deceit—
> let me be weighed in a just balance,
>> and let God know my integrity!—
> if my step has turned aside from the way,
>> and my heart has followed my eyes,
>> and if any spot has clung to my hands,
> then let me sow and another eat,
>> and let what grows for me be rooted out. (Job 31:5-8)

Job uses legal terminology and form to swear his innocence. Job is challenging God to appear and explain the charges against him.[6] In this oath of innocence, Job says, essentially, "If I have done this bad thing, then let this worse thing befall me." The if/then form provides a means for Job to put his accusers to the test. If the curses come to pass, then he is obviously guilty of the corresponding crime. If the curse does not happen, then it proves that he is legally innocent.[7] In this situation, God functions as both the witness and the judge of Job's declaration of innocence.[8] Job has yearned repeatedly, and loudly, for a chance to confront God. This oath creates a way for God to respond.[9] Even no response at all would be a response because if none of the curses happen, that would be evidence of Job's innocence. His oath pushes the legal metaphor to its limit and essentially demands an answer from God.

> O that I had one to hear me!
> (Here is my signature! Let the Almighty answer me!)
> O that I had the indictment written by my adversary! (Job 31:35)

---

[4]John E. Hartley, *The Book of Job* (Grand Rapids, MI: Eerdmans, 1988), 385.
[5]Dick, "The Legal Metaphor in Job 31," 47.
[6]Leo Perdue, *Wisdom in Revolt: Metaphorical Theology in the Book of Job* (Sheffield, UK: Sheffield Academic Press, 1991), 185.
[7]Perdue, *Wisdom in Revolt*, 183.
[8]J. Gerald Janzen, "Job's Oath," *Review and Expositor* no. 4 (Fall 2002): 599.
[9]Janzen, "Job's Oath," 603.

Job signs his complaint and submits it to God. And he doesn't have to wait long because the whirlwind is on the horizon.

JUSTICE

Job's focus on justice and vindication reminds us that one of the primary issues many trauma survivors may wrestle with concerns justice. As Cataldo writes, "Trauma survivors want reasons, they want justice, they want someone to be responsible."[10] This need for an answer to the question of why, why did this happen to me, why me, why am I going through this, coupled with a deep yearning for justice for what happened is understandable. Great injustice cries out for the scales to be righted. Job's struggle for vindication and justice resonates with trauma survivors who are also looking for justice in response to their own suffering.

This yearning for justice may be a significant struggle for some trauma survivors. Healing may seem impossible when the wound has never been acknowledged nor an apology ever given. Sometimes an apology isn't possible. The perpetrator may have passed away, or moved, or it simply isn't safe for the survivor to be near their abuser. Sometimes the perpetrator isn't sorry and might never repent, or the perpetrator may be so consumed with shame and their own pain that they can't bring themselves to take responsibility for their actions. Or perhaps the trauma is a response to a natural disaster, an accident, a medical diagnosis, the death of a loved one or another circumstance where there is no one responsible for the suffering, and no one to blame. What do we do when the responsible person shirks their responsibility to acknowledge the harm they caused? And what do we do when there is no one to blame? Both of these situations can complicate the healing process.

We see two important aspects of this need for justice play out in the book of Job. First, Job wants an answer from God. He wants to meet

---

[10]Lisa M. Cataldo, "I Know That My Redeemer Lives: Relational Perspectives on Trauma, Dissociation, and Faith," *Pastoral Psychology* 62, no. 6 (December 2013): 797.

God face-to-face in a courtroom and get a judgment. Job wants to be vindicated, declared innocent before God. He wants the injustice of his suffering acknowledged. We can trace that in the legal metaphor that runs through the text. The second aspect, however, is one we need to acknowledge and be aware of when we minister to trauma survivors. Notice that in this question of justice in the text, the friends lay the blame for Job's suffering on Job himself. Because they cannot face a challenge to their belief in retribution and the justice of God, they choose to blame the only other person available . . . Job. Job's friends turn their critical eyes to Job. Surely God would not be unjust therefore Job must deserve his suffering. Their instinct to protect their worldview leads them to place the blame on Job.

Now before we pile on the friends again for their insensitivity and terrible misunderstanding of the situation, let's look at their perspective. Job's words threaten their most fundamental beliefs about God, creation, and suffering. Job's first words in Job 3 were a curse against creation. Job's de-creation plea points to the de-creation of his inner world. His world has fallen apart so what possible order is there in the rest of the world? As he develops the legal metaphor throughout the text, Job also destabilizes the idea of justice in the world. There is an important connection here between justice and cosmic order.[11] For Job to assert that he has been treated unjustly is to challenge the entire system of cosmic order.[12] From this perspective, it is not surprising that the friends react so violently to Job's legal language and his quest for justice. For the friends, if Job is right, the entire created order is topsy-turvy. The only way to maintain their understanding of the world is to blame Job. They acknowledge that Job is suffering, but in order for their world to be just, Job must deserve that suffering and therefore he must have sinned. Anything else is absolutely untenable for the friends.

---

[11]Perdue, *Wisdom in Revolt*, 140.
[12]Perdue, *Wisdom in Revolt*, 140.

Passive Bystanders

The second element we see in the legal metaphor is the role of the passive bystander. Cataldo notes that "all trauma is experienced as having a 'passive bystander' who is implicated in the trauma."[13] Life rarely happens in a vacuum. We live our lives in community, usually multiple types of communities. We have our family, our work, our school, our church, our weekend hiking group, our playdate friends. Life happens in community. So, when trauma occurs, there are witnesses. There will be, hopefully, trusted listeners who hear and comfort us, but there will also be passive bystanders: those who witness, to some degree, the trauma-inducing event or the trauma response that follows, and do nothing. Those who know but refuse to act. Or worse, those who know but choose to stand with the perpetrator. When a trauma survivor reaches out for help and doesn't receive it or receives additional pain in the form of rejection, dismissal, blame, or condemnation instead, there is a second injury. The community the survivor trusted fails. In the book of Job, the friends fail to engage with Job's suffering and become perpetrators of a second injury as they inflict further wounding on him in their accusations and blame.[14] Job himself notes the failure of the friends to act as trusted listeners or compassionate others:

> As for you, you whitewash with lies;
>> all of you are worthless physicians.
> If you would only keep silent,
>> that would be your wisdom! (Job 13:4-5)
> I have heard many such things;
>> miserable comforters are you all. (Job 16:2)

Job's community fails him at the moment he needs them most.

---

[13]Cataldo, "I Know That My Redeemer Lives," 802.

[14]Ronnie Janoff-Bulman, *Shattered Assumptions: Towards a New Psychology of Trauma* (New York: The Free Press, 1992), 147.

Not only do Job's friends fail to listen and support him, they actively blame him for his situation. Victim blaming in the aftermath of a traumatic event may be rooted in the bystander's desire to preserve their fundamental assumptions about the world and sense of security in the world.[15] By blaming the victim for their circumstances, the passive bystander is, in effect, declaring themself to be immune from such circumstances because they would never make the same mistake. If the survivor is at fault for their circumstance, then the bystander, who has not done anything wrong, will not suffer the same fate. If, however, the bystander acknowledges the injustice of the suffering or admits that the survivor did not cause it or deserve it, then the bystander will be forced to confront their own vulnerability and insecurity in a chaotic and scary world. Victim blaming brings an illusion of control.

"What did she expect marrying that kind of man?"

"That's what happens when you ride that kind of bike/drive that kind of car."

"When you live in that area/go to that kind of place/wear that type of clothing. . . ."

"What did he/she think was going to happen?"

These types of victim-blaming and -shaming responses point to a desperate need for control and safety by the bystanders. If that terrible suffering happened to that person, then all I have to do to avoid suffering is not do what they did. If the bystander can identify what the victim did to cause or deserve their suffering, then they can breathe a sigh of relief because they would never do something like that.

Just like Job's friends, who couldn't confront the weaknesses in their theology, bystanders who seek to find fault in the victim as an explanation or justification of their suffering are attempting to keep a crooked world straight. They are trying to keep their beliefs about the

---

[15]Janoff-Bulman, *Shattered Assumptions*, 149.

world intact. They need to find a reason for the suffering so they are not confronted with an unreasonable world. Additionally, if these bystanders can point to the survivor's role in causing the trauma, the bystanders absolve themselves of the responsibility to help. "By blaming victims, people not only maintain their own illusions of invulnerability, but also minimize their sense of responsibility for helping."[16] The friends, in their evaluation of Job's suffering as a just result of his sins, have made a presumption of Job's guilt that not only explains the situation by blaming Job, but it also serves to allay their sense of responsibility for providing comfort and healing. For them, it is Job's responsibility to repent and fix the situation.

One of the subtle ways we see a version of this in many churches and Christian communities is in a misuse of Romans 8:28.

> We know that all things work together for good for those who love
> God, who are called according to his purpose.

Now, before you email me or send me critical DMs, let me say upfront, this is a beautiful verse of true and inspired Scripture. I believe it. I share it. I honor and respect it. I have also heard it too many times to count. When I walked through a dark and painful season, this verse more than any other was texted to me, written on cards, and repeated in phone calls. And while I appreciate the sentiment and I do, in fact, believe that God can redeem even the worst moments of our lives, in the context of trauma, we need to take a step back and evaluate why this is one of our go-to verses. Yes, it sounds hopeful and encouraging, but beneath those well-intentioned sentiments, we may be unintentionally shifting the burden and the blame back onto survivors. Are we telling them if they really loved God, if they just had enough faith, they would find the good in this tragedy and embrace it? We may be communicating that they should accept this unjust and unfair situation as God's plan for their life and be okay with it. Friends, in the midst of trauma healing,

---

[16]Janoff-Bulman, *Shattered Assumptions*, 150.

that may not be the most helpful approach. Survivors are not responsible for the trauma they endured, and they are not to be blamed for their trauma response. If we put the burden on the trauma survivor to reframe their experience as something positive that will benefit God's kingdom, we are effectively silencing them and dismissing their story. It may not be victim blaming, but it is definitely victim burdening.

In a stunning twist in the book of Job, God is also depicted at various times as a passive bystander who does not intervene on Job's behalf. This perceived change in relationship between Job and YHWH is one of the primary components of Job's trauma. In his suffering, Job sees God as both perpetrator and passive bystander.[17] As the perpetrator, God inflicts the suffering and as the passive bystander, God sees Job's suffering but refuses to step in and help. These two conflicting images make sense in light of what we know about the occasionally contradictory thoughts in trauma. Compare these verses:

> I will say to God, "Do not condemn me;
>> let me know why you contend against me." (Job 10:2)

In this verse, God is the perpetrator of Job's suffering, but in the verse below God is seen as the passive bystander.

> Even when I cry out, "Violence!" I am not answered;
>> I call aloud, but there is no justice. (Job 19:7)

Here, Job calls for justice, but receives no reply. God is thus the passive bystander whom Job is unable to move to response. The simultaneous presence of such contradictory conceptions of God highlights the fragmentary nature of trauma. For the trauma survivor, God may seem like a passive bystander who refuses to act on the survivor's behalf. They pray and cry and beg, but no answer seems to come. Or God may seem like the perpetrator causing their suffering. And for some, like Job, God may be both at the same time.

---

[17]Cataldo, "I Know That My Redeemer Lives," 801.

REVENGE FANTASIES

The third element in the legal metaphor that we will look at is the concept of the revenge fantasy. A revenge fantasy is when a trauma survivor imagines a way, or ways, to exact revenge on the person they hold responsible for their suffering. That imagined revenge may not be violent; it may be public humiliation, a public apology, a similar traumatic event befalling the perpetrator, or an uncovering of a secret sin that causes the perpetrator to experience loss. Judith Herman writes, "The desire for revenge also arises out of the experience of complete helplessness. In her humiliated fury, the victim imagines revenge is the only way to restore her own sense of power. She may also imagine that this is the only way to force the perpetrator to acknowledge the harm he has done to her."[18] The survivor who was harmed wants the perpetrator to experience the same type of harm, or worse. It is something of an eye-for-an-eye type of retribution. For survivors, the hope of the perpetrator experiencing suffering seems like a way for their own pain to be assuaged. The survivor may feel that in order for them to experience healing, the perpetrator needs to pay for what they've done. In the context of the legal metaphor, Job's lawsuit language may be seen as a way for Job to force YHWH to acknowledge Job's innocence. As Job repeatedly asks for an audience with God in order to present his case, there is an underlying desire for an acknowledgment of the harm that has been done.

Related to the revenge fantasy is the fantasy of compensation. Herman describes the compensation fantasy as "the desire for victory over the perpetrator that erases the humiliation of the trauma."[19] This compensation is ultimately more concerned with psychological compensation

---

[18]Judith Herman, *Trauma and Recovery: The Aftermath of Violence—from Domestic Abuse to Political Terror* (New York: Basic Books), 189. See also Judith Herman, *Truth and Repair: How Trauma Survivors Envision Justice* (New York: Basic Book, 2023). Herman's most recent work reiterates her earlier research on trauma, including the stages of healing discussed here and adds additional extensive research on justice and what justice means for trauma survivors.

[19]Herman, *Trauma and Recovery*, 190.

than material compensation.[20] It is a desire to be made whole again, to get back something that was lost. In Job's legal metaphor, he seeks vindication and legal clearance. This vindication would be a form of compensation. Notably, Job, in his lawsuit, does not demand restitution for his losses, rather his focus is on a declaration of his innocence.

What we need to recognize as survivors and comforters is that both revenge fantasies and compensation fantasies are rooted in the idea of justice. A revenge or compensation fantasy is not bitterness nor a lack of maturity nor an inability to forgive. It is a normal and expected response and may play a part in trauma healing. However, the language a survivor uses may be shocking. Imagine Job's friends hearing their suffering friend say that he wants to sue God. Hearing a survivor in our church say they want a perpetrator to lose everything may be alarming to us. Hearing a survivor say they want their abuser to be hit by a car might shock us. However, understanding trauma reminds us that this is not an unusual response. The survivor wants justice and if the community or society can't, or won't, provide it, their imagination may fill in the gap. Now, there is clearly an important difference between a survivor's normal desire for their pain to be lessened by seeing their perpetrator brought to justice or receiving some form of compensation and a survivor actively planning to hurt someone. As comforters and trusted witnesses we need to exercise discernment and wisdom in differentiating between the two and recognize when outside professional help is needed.

The idea of revenge and compensation fantasies as part of a trauma response is important for us to be aware of, especially as Christians who are deeply formed by forgiveness. Forgiveness is a cornerstone of our faith. We stand before God forgiven and redeemed because of the finished work of Jesus Christ on the cross. We hear about forgiveness all the time. From the pulpit, in our small groups, in Christian

---

[20]Herman, *Trauma and Recovery*, 190.

books, podcasts, and conferences. But, as vital as forgiveness is to our faith and our walk with God, forgiveness can be weaponized and turned against a wounded and hurting person. There is a time for forgiveness, but there is also a time for grief, anger, sadness, and sorrow. Again, the right answer at the wrong time is still the wrong answer. While our desire to help a survivor get to a place of forgiveness might be right, we have to be sensitive to the sometimes lengthy process of trauma healing. Imagine if we were called to the bedside of someone who had lost part of their leg in a tragic accident. Picture their leg still bandaged from surgery, their eyes glassy with shock at looking down and seeing only empty space. Even if the doctor had told us that the patient would be able to walk with assistance, that there are all kinds of prosthetic options and that they may be able to ride a bike someday, in that moment of loss and shock, we wouldn't tell them to hop out of bed and start adapting to their new life. There is a time for that, but it isn't then. The same is true for trauma. There may be a time for forgiveness, but we need to be sensitive to that fact that it will be on the survivor's timeline and when they are ready, not when we want them to be ready. Pressuring a survivor to forgive is another example of burden-shifting. It places a burden and an expectation on an already-wounded person and conveys the idea that if the survivor cannot or chooses not to forgive in that moment then they are now to blame for something. It creates a tension where if the survivor does not forgive on our timeline we are implying that their continued pain, suffering, or hardship is their fault because they refused the solution we provided.

And here's the part where you may get mad at me . . . we also have to be aware of our own agenda behind the forgiveness discussion. Why do we want the survivor to forgive? Is it because we truly believe that it is the best next step in their healing? Or is it because we want the situation to be resolved? Are we anxious for the survivor to forgive so any lingering awkwardness can be set aside, and everyone can move on? As comforters, it is unfortunately easy to put pressure on the survivor to heal rather than accepting our need to be patient. We see their trauma response as something to be fixed as quickly as possible. With (hopefully) the best of intentions, we want the survivor to hurry up and be okay. If we can get them to forgive, then our work is done. But this idea that the survivor forgiving their perpetrator is some sort of finish line we are running toward can be destructive and damaging. It conveys the idea that once a survivor says those magic words "I forgive . . ." the situation is over and done never to be revisited again. If, as survivors, we later bring it up again, we might hear, "But you've already forgiven him/her/them. Why are you still bringing it up?" As comforters, we want to push and press a survivor to cross that imaginary finish line, but then we refuse to let them go back ever again, even if there are still pieces of the trauma they need to resolve. The tension can be suffocating. On the one hand we tell them that they need to forgive, they are commanded to forgive, they have to forgive, and when they do, we tell them they aren't allowed to bring it up again. You forgave that person so it's in the past. If you keep bringing it up, you're holding on to bitterness or refusing to let it go. Do you see the catch-22 here? Survivors may find themselves in a no-win situation. And this catch-22 may also be framed by the contradiction where we expect a survivor to forgive, but we fail to expect the perpetrator to acknowledge their actions and make amends to the person they hurt.

Forgiveness is a beautiful gift. It is grace and compassion and kindness and love. It is all of those things. It also isn't easy. If we can struggle to forgive someone who cuts us off in traffic, imagine trying to forgive the person who nearly destroyed you and never even acknowledged your pain. Walking with the hurting is walking on scarred ground. We must tread lightly around wounds that are not ours. It is not our pain to fix, and it is not our trauma to resolve. In the community of faith, we have the opportunity to sit with the broken, hold hands with the grieving and the bind the wounds of the hurting. To speak words that lead to healing we need to be mindful of the reality of trauma and steward the trust of survivors well.

LESSONS LEARNED

- Many trauma survivors long for justice. This may be as simple as an apology or as complex as a jail term. The yearning for justice after suffering wounding is an understandable response.

- We cannot force survivors to forgive when they are not ready to do so. Forgiveness is not a finish line for us to reach.

- Often victim-blaming and victim-burdening responses are attempts for witnesses to feel in control of a situation and convince themselves that they are protected from such suffering.

REFLECTION QUESTIONS

- Is there a wounding or betrayal in your past that you are still waiting to receive an apology for? What would it feel like to hear the words "I'm sorry"?

- How would you describe forgiveness? What does forgiveness mean for you in your own life?

- What would justice look like for Job? What is he longing for?

SEVEN

OUT OF THE WHIRLWIND

You know that moment in a movie or television show when the main character is talking to a friend and giving a scathing indictment of another character, absolutely ripping them to shreds, detailing their flaws and foibles in excruciating detail, when suddenly the eyes of the person they're talking to get wide and filled with terror and the main character stops and says in a resigned voice, "They're standing right behind me, aren't they?" I imagine the voice of YHWH speaking from the whirlwind hit Job a bit like that. Job has spent the past thirty-six chapters growing more and more upset, demanding an audience with God, and then with a churning of the wind and the howling of a wild storm, YHWH shows up.

That scene has always filled me with awe and wonder. In the midst of Job's pain, in the ash heap of his suffering, God shows up. God doesn't wait for Job to have all his stuff together. God is not standing far off and waiting for Job to dust himself off and crawl his way over. God meets Job right where he is. Smack dab in the middle of the pain, anger, suffering, and oozing sores, God comes to the ashes and speaks to Job. There is something so beautiful about our incarnational God.

God comes to us. Jesus was born in a manager; the Son of God left heaven to dwell in our midst, to suffer in our midst, and to rise again in our midst. Imagine what that would mean for Job who has been exiled from his community and has been alone in the ash heap, consumed by loss, pain, and grief. His friends have turned on him, blamed him for his suffering, and pressured him to repent of made-up crimes. Then God shows up.

It doesn't require a huge stretch of the imagination for most of us to know what that feels like. What it feels like when we have fallen and someone reaches out their hand to help us. What it feels like when we are lonely, and someone calls to check on us. When we are struggling, and someone leaves a box of groceries on our doorstep. When we are alone and scared in the hospital and someone stops by to sit with us. To be seen, heard, and loved in the middle of the darkness and ashes, that is a precious gift. It is one Job's friends could have brought, but in their theological debates and condemnation they missed it. The church has the chance every day to be this kind of community, but sadly we, like Job's friends, also often miss it. We miss the call to be the hand of help because we are too wrapped up in our business decisions, growth conferences, and platform building. We are willing to sacrifice the one because we want to reach the thousand. We become so busy protecting our institutions that we ignore the one who is hurting right under our own roof. We exile them, metaphorically speaking, to the ashes because we don't want them to track dirt on our freshly shampooed carpet. We rush past our own hurting people to put on a show for visitors so we can fill up a building and, in the process, we forget the church is not a building at all. The church is people, bruised, broken, messy people who are turning to us for help, wisdom, and love. We as pastors, church leaders, and believers are then faced with a choice . . . will we join the ranks of Job's friends and be miserable comforters or will we be comforters in the ashes?

THE MEANING OF TRAUMA

By the time we get to Job 38, we have been through the wringer. It has been an emotional and exhausting ride. Then suddenly this happens:

Then the LORD answered Job out of the whirlwind:

"Who is this that darkens counsel by words without knowledge?
Gird up your loins like a man;
I will question you, and you shall declare to me." (Job 38:1-3)

God is on the scene. And what follows is a whirlwind tour of creation as YHWH responds to Job. I'm not going to sugarcoat it; the divine speeches in the book of Job are complex. There is no scholarly consensus on what they mean or even how God spoke them. Was God being a bully? Was God being sarcastic? Was God being a gentle teacher? It is a scholarly muddle of conflicting opinions and interpretations. So let me lay my cards on the table. I don't have all the answers about what these divine speeches mean. After spending years studying the book of Job, I have my opinions, and not everyone will agree with me, but the one thing I want to concentrate on in this book is what these divine speeches mean for Job, and what they mean for the church in ministering to trauma survivors. We'll certainly cover some of the controversial issues, but we'll be focusing primarily on how the divine speeches help Job resolve his trauma and rejoin his community.[1]

First, I want to make a quick distinction between meaning and meaning-making space. One of the needs many trauma survivors have is to be able to make sense of their traumatic experience. They need to give it meaning. Most of us recognize that we can deal with almost anything if it makes sense to us—if there is meaning and purpose

---

[1]As I said in the beginning, there isn't space in this book to cover all of the interpretive issues in the book of Job. Fortunately, there are many insightful and learned scholars who have undertaken extensive study of the book of Job. If you are interested in digging into more of the complexities of the text or some of the sections and issues I had to skip over, I recommend starting with the commentaries that have already been mentioned as well as the other resources included in the bibliography.

behind it. It's when something hits us out of left field and doesn't make any sense at all that we often struggle to deal with the event in a healthy manner. Assigning meaning to a traumatic experience is one step that can help in putting the trauma response to rest. Because of the fragmentary characteristic of traumatic memories, it can be difficult to find meaning in the mess of the disorganized snippets of memory. Those memories need to be put together in a coherent narrative so the survivor can begin to process the event and eventually give it meaning. Once the survivor has a narrative of the event, it can still be a challenge to understand the why. Why did this happen? Why did it happen to me? What does it mean? As survivors, we need mental space to work through this meaning-making process and rebuild our broken window. It is in the divine speeches that we see most clearly the rebuilding of Job's shattered inner world. Within this rebuilding, Job is finally able to resolve his trauma and leave the ash heap.

What we find, then, in the book of Job is not so much a theological answer for why suffering happens so much as a meaning-making space within which Job is able to heal and resume his life as a servant of YHWH. It is within this meaning-making space in the text that Job is able to integrate his traumatic experience into a new more comprehensive worldview. Job rebuilds a window that has meaning, even if the author never tells us specifically what Job thinks that meaning is. All we know for sure is that it is within this space that Job encounters YHWH, and after that encounter he is able to reconstruct his shattered world. In this divine encounter, Job receives what he personally needs to resolve his trauma, which allows him to rise from the ash heap, return to his life, and reconnect with society. There are no easy answers here, no straightforward explanations, but that is trauma for you. There won't always be a quick and easy answer, and sometimes the steps a survivor needs to take may not make sense to us as trusted witnesses, but it will be exactly what they needed to heal.

After the divine speeches, the poetry section ends, and the prose epilogue begins. Job is once again a valued member of his community. He is able to leave his trauma, symbolized by the ash heap, behind and engage again in his family and community life as demonstrated by his intercession for the friends, his interaction with community members, and the naming of his daughters. The problem for many scholars and readers is that this resolution does not seem satisfactory. Job never receives an explanation for his suffering. No one ever tells him, "Hey, by the way there was this debate in heaven and you ended up going through serious suffering because of it." Job leaves the ash heap still not knowing why this all happened to him, and yet he is able resolve his trauma. This tension has led to centuries of analysis and debate on the meaning of the book of Job as whole and the divine speeches in particular.

The sad truth is that much of trauma is inexplicable. There are countless traumatic events that can never and will never be adequately explained. This is especially apparent in our post-Holocaust world. There may be lots of theories, lots of reasons, and analyses of what led to such an atrocity, but the reality is there are some things that simply cannot be explained. This is certainly the case in the book of Job. While we, as readers, got to listen in on the heavenly council and see the behind-the-scenes machinations that led to Job's suffering, Job himself is never given this information. Even when conversing with YHWH, Job is never told why he suffered as he did. Yet, after this encounter, even in the absence of explanation, Job is able to rebuild his cognitive schemas in a way that enables him to reconcile with YHWH while also recognizing the reality of his experience of unjust suffering. Therefore, it cannot be explanation that lies at the heart of resolving trauma in the book of Job. Job does not receive an explanation, but he is still able to resolve his trauma and find meaning in his world again.

As Job's tangible world is shaken and destroyed, his inner world similarly falls apart. His window is shattered, nothing makes sense anymore. Job is ultimately confronted by a world that, for him, has lost its meaning. Job's primary struggle was not simply the magnitude of his losses, great though they were, but it was also the collapse of meaning the losses precipitated, including his perceived loss of his relationship with YHWH, his belief in a fundamental order in the universe, and his trust in the justice of God. Job's world becomes fundamentally unmoored, as reflected in his de-creation plea in Job 3. There is no order, no predictability, and no stability any longer in his world. For Job, the world becomes, essentially, meaningless. He cannot move forward, and he cannot rejoin the community because he exists in a disordered and chaotic world that lacks meaning. This connection between meaning and order is also seen in the reaction of Job's friends. As they encourage him to repent in order to be restored, they are reflecting the idea that "if the victim can be blamed for what happened, then the world is not a random, malevolent, meaningless place. Rather it is a place in which outcomes are contingent upon who you are and what you do."[2] Justice and order go hand in hand. From the friends' perspective, if Job's suffering is his fault, then there is order in the world. If he is not responsible for the suffering he has endured, if the losses and devastation that afflicted him were not warranted by his sin, then there is no right ordering in the world.

Yet, in these concluding chapters of the book, YHWH appears on the scene and speaks order into the chaos. It is significant and powerful that when YHWH speaks, the language is of the same type Job used when he first began to speak in Job 3. If we remember all the way back to that chapter, Job launches the poetry section with creation language. For Job, it is de-creation language and imagery, but it is rooted in the idea of creation. Job's world has fallen apart, and his language reflects that. Job's ordered world has descended into chaos. When the voice of God speaks from the whirlwind, God not only meets Job right where he is in the ash heap of his suffering, God also uses the same type of language as Job . . . the language of creation. God uses creation language to bring order to the chaos of Job's trauma. What Job declared

---

[2]Ronnie Janoff-Bulman, *Shattered Assumptions: Towards a New Psychology of Trauma* (New York: The Free Press, 1992), 149.

to be de-created and chaotic, YHWH declares to be created and ordered. YHWH is rebuilding the cognitive world Job had lost.

Job had been engaging in schema testing throughout the dialogue cycles. He has tried on different metaphors and different explanations to try to make sense out of his experience. It is here, in the divine speeches, that Job finally finds an explanatory schema that works. It is as if he had been rearranging the broken fragments and shards of his window, laying them out on the carpet in different patterns and designs, cutting himself on the edges a few times, trying again and again to find a way to fit them all together and then suddenly, in the whirlwind, he gets it. He knows how to put the pieces back together. In his encounter with YHWH, Job finds a new image for his window, he finds a new mosaic that will hold all the pieces, an image that can enfold everything he has experienced and allow him to leave the ashes of his trauma.

It Is Their Trauma, Not Ours

Just as a trauma survivor has to figure out how to enfold their experience into their understanding of the world and their place in it, comforters must often do the same thing. We hear about something terrible happening, we watch someone struggle with a horrific event, and we need to figure out where that goes in *our* mental filing cabinet. What do we think of it? How does it impact our understanding of God, the world, and our place in it? What does it mean? The temptation here is for us to think through it, assign meaning to the event, and then decide that our meaning is the correct one. We may have all kinds of theology and Bible verses to back up our opinion, but even with all of that, and even if our explanation lines up with our faith and doctrine, it still may not be the meaning the survivor finds in their experience. Sitting with someone who is healing from trauma can stir up all kinds of reactions in those who serve as comforters. As trusted listeners and comforters we must be mindful of our own responses and emotional reactions. As Henri Nouwen pointed out, we are all "wounded healers."[3] None of us are perfect and none of us have all the answers. But we are all capable of showing love, support, and presence.

As we minister to trauma survivors, we must also keep the context of the trauma in mind. Trauma can be both individual and collective. It is important that we recognize both types of responses and be aware of how they may intersect. An individual trauma is an experience that affects one person and triggers a trauma response for them. Like Job. Job individually suffered staggering losses. While his wife no doubt also suffered from the terrible losses that take place, the book of Job is focused on Job and so we see in the text an example of individual trauma . . . though someone really should have been checking on Job's wife, too. An individual trauma may be a devastating injury or medical diagnosis, combat experience, sexual assault, spiritual abuse, losing a child, the list can go on and on. It is essentially an experience that is centered on an individual. Collective trauma, on the other hand, is a community-wide event. It is a traumatic event that affects an entire community, culture, or people group. Contemporary examples would include 9/11, the 2004 tsunami, the Rwandan genocide, the Holocaust, and the COVID-19 pandemic. It is an event that impacts a community and is not limited to an individual. We see examples of collective trauma in the Hebrew Bible in the enslavement of the Israelites in Egypt, stories of widespread famine, and the Babylonian captivity. In these situations, an entire community suffered a traumatic event that eventually becomes a part of the community's story and identity.

Just like in individual trauma, in a collective trauma experience, the community needs to find meaning in the event. The community looks for an explanation and a purpose in the event. In the Hebrew Bible we see this explanatory endeavor in postexilic literature that explains the Babylonian captivity as a just punishment for the nation's sins. This story carries explanatory power, and it becomes an agreed-on narrative

---

[3]Henri Nouwen, *The Wounded Healer: Ministry in Contemporary Society* (New York: Doubleday Religion, 2010).

that gives meaning to the catastrophic event. The community, in this case the nation of Judah, accepts the narrative that the exile was a just punishment that leads them to return to YHWH. It becomes a collective story of the nation. In this collective trauma, the wider community seeks an explanatory story that can be adopted and embraced by the majority of the group. The difficulty is that this agreed-on explanation may overwrite, or ignore, the experience of an individual within that group, even if the traumatic event is the same. In other words, an individual within the community may have had a different experience of the traumatic event. The story the community adopts to explain the trauma may not fit with the individual's experience, but in order to preserve the community, the individual story must be set aside. This is, in effect, what Job's friends set out to do. Though the book of Job is not a story of community-wide trauma, what we see in the friends' responses is a collective explanation of suffering that is threatened by Job's individual experience, an explanation that alienates and isolates Job.

This need for a generally accepted cultural story also plays out in the modern church. Think about the last time you personally experienced something distressing. It might not have risen to the level of a trauma response, but something that caused you sorrow or grief or anger. Did you share that with a trusted Christian friend or leader? And did you hear one (or all) of the following?

"You know, God works all things together for good. . . ."
"God says he knows the plans he has for you. . . ."
"God will turn your mourning into dancing. . . ."
"This test will become your testimony. . . ."
"God calls us to forgive even when it's hard. . . ."

Every single one of those statements may be true (contextual issues aside). But every one of those statements can also be an example of a collective story response to an individual trauma. Often, we, in the church, want to hold on to our explanations of suffering in the world no matter the cost. When we are confronted with someone else's trauma, we may be tempted to offer them our standard, go-to explanation. We want, surely with the best of intentions, to guide them to the "right" answer and get them back to "normal" as quickly as possible. If they will simply accept the explanation we provide they can forgive, move on, and let it go. If the survivor resists this narrative or challenges it or simply can't accept it, we may view them as a problem to be fixed. The collective story must be upheld so we attempt to silence the survivor. We see this in the book of Job when the hot-headed Elihu comes right out and says it:

> Pay heed, Job, listen to me;
> > be silent, and I will speak.
> If you have anything to say, answer me;
> > speak, for I desire to justify you.
> If not, listen to me;
> > be silent, and I will teach you wisdom. (Job 33:31-33)

In our churches today, the silencing of a survivor may not be quite as obvious as Elihu's words, but the effect might be the same. Anytime we try to impose an explanation on a survivor we run the risk of silencing them in order to preserve our collective story. We don't want our agreed-on narrative challenged so we view any disagreement or resistance as a threat to be neutralized. We end up confronting survivors with a "get on board" choice. Either they conform to our narrative and accept the meaning we impose, or they get labeled as the problem. When the problem comes from within the church itself, from abuses in leadership or destructive and toxic cultures, this pressure to follow the script is magnified as it becomes a crisis of existence for the institution. Too often, to protect the institution or to protect the charismatic leader the institution depends on, the survivor is silenced, dismissed, or kicked out.

Hopefully, putting it in such stark terms demonstrates the danger in this approach. Do we want to be good teachers and counselors? Of course. Do we want to uphold sound doctrine? Yes. But trauma is messy and sometimes we need to put our neat and tidy explanations aside and dig into the mud with the survivor to help them find their own way out. In an individual trauma, the survivor needs the opportunity and freedom to craft their own narrative in order to integrate the traumatic experience into their life story and mental schemas.[4] Any attempt to bury an individual survivor's experience into the broader community narrative denies the survivor their voice and the opportunity to process and integrate their trauma in their own way. This empowering of a survivor's story may require us to be comfortable with ambiguity. Sometimes the explanations and stories we cling to simply don't work . . . or they don't work yet. Survivors and witnesses may never get all the answers to why a traumatic event occurred, and we need to be okay with that. The goal isn't an answer, the goal is healing.

What Does It All Mean?

By the time we get to the divine speeches in Job 38–41, we are ready for some answers. God shows up in a whirlwind and we are ready for an explanation. I bet Job was too. After going round and round with his miserable comforter friends, Job finally gets what he has been asking for, an audience with God. Job has challenged God to a lawsuit and God shows up. But what God says in these divine speeches is not at all what we expect. There is no legal defense, there is no explanation for why Job suffered, God doesn't address any of Job's questions. Instead, God shows up and says, "I've got some questions for you, Job." But somehow after these two speeches by YHWH, Job is able to leave the ash heap and rejoin his community. There is something in these speeches, something in this encounter with God that allows Job to resolve his trauma.

The question is what?

The book of Job centers on Job's experience of trauma, an experience that leads him to theological questioning and an eventual encounter

---

[4]David Janzen, "Claimed and Unclaimed Experience: Problematic Readings of Trauma in the Hebrew Bible," *Biblical Interpretation* 27, no. 2 (2019): 165.

with YHWH. God does not explain Job's suffering, nor is there a grand theological explanation for all suffering in the world. Neither does Job explain to us what he learns in this transformative encounter. What we find instead is a meaning-making space that gives Job the opportunity to express and understand his experience, even without receiving an explanation. The absence of any explanation at all does not negate the resolution of the traumatic experience. Instead, it highlights the priority of resolution over explanation. A trauma survivor can heal from trauma without ever receiving an explanation for their suffering. This is, in fact, what occurs in the book of Job. Job is never given a reason for his experience. He is never told about the behind-the-scenes heavenly discussions that led to his trauma. He is, however, given in the encounter with God the necessary means to rebuild his inner schemas and move forward with a worldview that can encompass both his personal experience of trauma and his theology.

We have seen that God meets Job in the ashes of his suffering and dwells with him there. God descends into the chaos of Job's experience and brings order. The language YHWH uses reflects the same creation imagery that Job used in Job 3. This connection not only honors Job's words and his struggle, but it also brings a level of understanding and intimacy in the conversation. YHWH demonstrates that he has heard what Job has been saying and is willing to participate in the conversation. Now, in all fairness, YHWH has plenty to say and correct. He doesn't show up with flowers and a candygram for Job, but neither does God show up with a gavel and condemn him. Instead, God meets Job in his pain, acknowledges that he has heard Job's anguish and his words, and then brings a perspective only God can bring. YHWH does not silence Job, rather YHWH reframes the conversation and guides Job into a rebuilding of his shattered world. It is the presence of God that leads Job to healing.

We should hopefully see a connection here with how we as comforters meet with trauma survivors. Their world has fallen apart, and so that is where we must go. We meet them where they are and participate in *their* conversation rather than trying to force them into ours. This should not come as surprise to any of us, but we are not God. Even on our best days, we do not have the omniscient, eternal, whirlwind perspective that God does. What we do have, however, is the ability to meet with survivors in the midst of their pain, listen to their story, and prayerfully help usher them into the presence of God. As we pray with them, and for them, we create space for their encounter with the One who can comfort, teach, guide, and heal them. Our task is not to have all the answers, but rather to help point them to the One who does.

There are two primary things I want to point out in the divine speeches. First, the divine speeches allow Job to rebuild his shattered schemas. Second, Job's response reflects a resolution of trauma. We'll cover these two issues in this chapter and in the following one. If Job's de-creation imagery reflected the collapse and destruction of his inner schemas, then it makes sense that YHWH's creation language demonstrates a rebuilding of those schemas. Job's experience of suffering has shattered his established worldview . . . his window has been broken. His framework for understanding the world has fallen apart. This is the nature of trauma. In order for the trauma to be resolved, he must rebuild those failed schemas into something more resilient. Job's previous schemas no longer hold because they proved to be incapable of reconciling undeserved suffering and a just God. Something new must be rebuilt. As Janoff-Bulman writes, "Survivors of traumatic events seek to arrive at a new, nonthreatening assumptive world, one that acknowledges and integrates their negative experience and prior illusions."[5] YHWH's creation language provides the tools for that rebuilding.

Trauma shakes a survivor to the core. When their schemas fail, the world seems hopelessly disordered and unsafe. "[Traumatic experiences] create a sense of alienation and disconnection so profound that

---

[5] Janoff-Bulman, *Shattered Assumptions*, 117.

the meaning of life, indeed the meaning of the entire created order, seems irrevocably shattered."[6] Job's world has fallen apart. It has resulted in trauma that has effectively rendered his world meaningless, disordered, and chaotic. This is reflected in his de-creation language in Job 3. The theme is then picked up by YHWH in Job 38. Where Job called for destruction, YHWH speaks life. Let's look at a specific comparison. In Job 9, Job says,

> He [God] removes mountains, and they do not know it
>   when he overturns them in his anger;
> he shakes the earth out of its place,
>   and its pillars tremble. (Job 9:5-6)

But in some of the first words YHWH speaks from the whirlwind, YHWH says,

> Where were you when I laid the foundation of the earth?
>   Tell me, if you have understanding.
> Who determined its measurements—surely you know!
>   Or who stretched the line upon it?
> On what were its bases sunk,
>   or who laid its cornerstone
> when the morning stars sang together
>   and all the heavenly beings shouted for joy? (Job 38:4-7)

In these words, YHWH recognizes the primordial chaos Job invoked and flips it around. It is especially evident in the image of YHWH setting the bases and cornerstone in place. This seems like a direct response to Job's earlier words that YHWH removes mountains and shakes the pillars. Job experiences chaos in the wake of his trauma, but YHWH steps in and brings order. YHWH's creation language helps Job see beyond the chaos he has experienced and reminds Job that creation, as a whole, is still ordered. God is still in control and

---

[6]Samuel Balentine, "Legislating Divine Trauma," in *Bible Through the Lens of Trauma*, ed. Elizabeth Boase and Christopher Frechette (Atlanta: SBL Press, 2016), 161.

chaos does not reign unchecked. As Job is able to see that his life is still contained within God's control, he is able to begin rebuilding his shattered window. YHWH's symbolic rebuilding of a broken world has an important resonance with the rebuilding of Job's shattered assumptions. As Baldwin writes, "Trauma is not the end of *the* world; but it is the end of *a* world."[7] Job's world was shattered, but YHWH is able to create a new one, a cognitive world that is capable of enfolding both suffering and faith. For trauma survivors their cognitive world has been shattered, and sometimes their physical world has been shattered as well if the traumatic event has resulted in injury, divorce, legal consequences, financial devastation, or other life-altering circumstances. And while the broader world spins on, it can be difficult to see order, purpose, and safety in the midst of the chaos of their pain.

Notice that we are talking about the building of a new world . . . symbolically speaking. Job cannot go back to his old schemas. He can never go back to the way things were. The trauma he has endured has changed everything. The impulse we may have when sitting with a trauma survivor to get them back to "normal" as soon as possible, to get them back to their old life, may be misguided. Trauma changes things. There is no going back. We can't unsee what we have seen. We have torn back the veil on suffering, and it can never be covered up again. That is why it is so important that we exhibit compassion and curiosity when dealing with trauma survivors. As much as we may want them to be able to "go back to the way things were," that may be the wrong hope. We want them to be able to move forward into the way things are. The old window won't do anymore; they need to build a new one and they need support and care in the process.

Job's experience of trauma created a need for a reconstruction of his inner schemas. What existed prior to his suffering is no longer valid. In spite of the friends' attempts to defend these preexisting beliefs, Job

---

[7] Jennifer Baldwin, *Trauma-Sensitive Theology: Thinking Theologically in the Era of Trauma* (Eugene, OR: Cascade Books, 2018), 30 (emphasis original).

cannot hold on to them any longer. Jones points out that for many trauma survivors this rethinking and reformation cannot be accomplished in isolation. It often requires an outside influence to intervene and suggest a different view of reality.[8] It's a bit like when we get stuck on a problem and we can't seem to find a solution until someone else shows up and flips the paper around. Sometimes, it is that outside influence that can propel a survivor to begin to see things differently. YHWH's appearance in the whirlwind breaks through Job's processing quagmire.

As we have seen, the dialogues between Job and his friends have gone around in circles. With the appearance of a fourth friend, Elihu, the cycle threatens to keep repeating. Elihu shows up after Job's oath of innocence and his words sound like a return to the dialogue process. The whole cycle is close to repeating, but instead, the dialogue is interrupted by YHWH himself. Instead of a repetition of the earlier cycle of friend speaks, Job speaks, friend speaks, Job speaks, the repetition is put to a stop with the appearance of YHWH. His words offer a startlingly new way of looking at the situation, one that answers the chaotic destruction of Job's world. YHWH's speeches are a far cry from the repeated calls by the friends for Job to repent and return to previous schemas that have already failed. In the divine speeches, YHWH provides a new way for Job to rethink and reform his fundamental beliefs.

EMPOWERING SURVIVORS

One of the most damaging aspects of trauma can be the feeling of helplessness and powerlessness that often accompanies it. As survivors, so much of trauma is outside of our control. It is very likely we had no agency in and no control over the event that precipitated the trauma response. It may have been a natural disaster or the choices of another person that were inflicted on us. An event overtook us and overwhelmed our nervous system. Even now, we may not have control of our trauma

---

[8]Serene Jones, *Trauma and Grace: Theology in a Ruptured World* (Louisville, KY: Westminster John Knox, 2019), xv.

response as memories and flashbacks appear without warning, anxiety spirals in seemingly ordinary situations, hypervigilance keeps us on edge, and we struggle to keep up with life. As survivors, we may feel helpless and powerless. It makes sense then that restoring agency and a sense of control can be helpful in trauma resolution. However, often a church community may respond to trauma by shuffling a survivor into the shadows, removing them from positions of leadership, taking them off volunteer teams all in a well-intentioned desire to give them time to heal. While there is a need to be compassionately aware of a survivor's need for space and to be sensitive to the pressures that might be weighing on a survivor, there is also a need to recognize the need for community, fellowship, and contribution in trauma healing. As with all aspects of ministering to trauma survivors, this shows the need for personal connection and intimacy. We can only discern the best way to support a survivor if we meet them where they are and minister according to their needs, not according to an unexamined application of procedure and policy.

The feeling of powerlessness that often accompanies a traumatic experience coupled with the loss of a sense of order and meaning in the world can undermine a survivor's ability to engage with society and their ability to recognize that they can exercise control and have purpose in the world. In the book of Job, the divine speeches reiterate and restore confidence in the divine order of the cosmos. This restoration of order speaks to a deep-felt need of Job as a trauma survivor. YHWH speaks from the whirlwind and points Job to the fundamental order of the universe. It is not the universe that has become disordered, rather it is Job's perception of it that needs to be rebuilt, a process that begins in the rhetorical questions of the divine speeches. YHWH's rhetorical questions are not solely displays of power or demeaning questions meant to belittle Job into submission.[9] Rather these questions invite Job to refocus

---

[9]Though some scholars disagree and see the divine speeches as exactly that. For such a perspective, see, for example, David Wolfers, *Deep Things Out of Darkness: The Book of Job Essays and a New English Translation* (Grand Rapids, MI: Eerdmans, 1995).

his thinking and actively participate in the rebuilding of his most deeply held assumptions about the world.[10] YHWH does not expect an answer from Job to the each of the questions, for each of the answers is obvious.[11] The purpose of the rhetorical questions is not new information, but the new integration of information Job already knows. It is the process of questioning that allows Job to become an active participant in an encounter with YHWH. YHWH does not preach to Job from a far-off place, instead YHWH enters into the ruins of Job's world and converses with him there.[12] This is not a forceful imposition of an explanation, but an intimate encounter that takes place on the ash heap of Job's shattered world. These questions allow Job to be a participant in his own healing. He is given a role to play in the process, a sense of control and agency in the midst of his feelings of powerlessness.

After this first divine speech, Job responds:

> Then Job answered the LORD:
>
> "See, I am of small account; what shall I answer you?
>> I lay my hand on my mouth.
> I have spoken once, and I will not answer,
>> twice but will proceed no further." (Job 40:3-5)

We see here that Job is on the road to healing. He has heard the voice of God and Job chooses to stop protesting. He will withdraw his lawsuit. But such a withdrawal does not seem to indicate a resolution of his trauma or a reconciliation in his relationship with God. Ortlund writes of Job's response after the first divine speech, "However good it is for Job

---

[10]This view is, of course, only one viable interpretation in a sea of interpretations proposed for the role of questions in the divine speeches. For other interpretive suggestions, see John E. Hartley, *The Book of Job* (Grand Rapids, MI: Eerdmans, 1988), 49; John H. Walton, *Job: The NIV Application Commentary* (Grand Rapids, MI: Zondervan, 2012), 399; Carol Newsom, "The Book of Job," in *The New Interpreters Bible*, vol. 4 (Nashville: Abingdon Press, 1996), 596; Leo Perdue, *Wisdom in Revolt: Metaphorical Theology in the Book of Job* (Sheffield, UK: Sheffield Academic Press, 1991), 205; Wolfers, *Deep Things Out of Darkness*, 209; Michael V. Fox, "God's Answer and Job's Response," *Biblica* 94, no. 1 (2013): 13.

[11]Fox, "God's Answer and Job's Response," 4.

[12]Kathleen O'Connor, *Job* (Collegeville, MN: Liturgical Press, 2012), 88.

to withdraw his protest, doing so does not in itself imply a healing of the distance between God and Job and a complete resolution of Job's trauma."[13] Ortlund's quote illustrates the progressive nature of healing from trauma. While the first divine speech and Job's response to it seem to indicate a movement toward healing, as Job ceases his vocal protests, the full resolution of his trauma has not yet taken place. It will take a second divine speech for Job to reconstruct the new schemas he requires to resolve his trauma and allow for a reconciliation between Job and YHWH.

LESSONS LEARNED

- After Job's encounter with YHWH in the divine speeches, Job is able to leave the ash heap and rejoin his community. Job finds resolution for his trauma in this encounter, even though what exactly it means to Job is never explicitly explained.

- Trauma survivors often experience feelings of helplessness and loss of control. Empowering survivors can help restore a sense of personal agency and efficacy in the world.

- Every trauma is a unique story. As comforters, we cannot rely on rehearsed answers or one-size fits all advice. Every survivor has a voice and a story to tell.

REFLECTION QUESTIONS

- When you read the divine speeches in the book of Job, what do you think YHWH is saying?

- Trauma leaves us changed. Is there an experience in your life that has left its mark on you and changed you? What did your life look like before and what does it look like now?

- How can a church community help empower survivors who may be struggling with feelings of helplessness or powerlessness?

---

[13]Eric Ortlund, *Piercing Leviathan: God's Defeat of Evil in the Book of Job* (Downers Grove, IL: InterVarsity Press, 2021), 103.

EIGHT

BEHEMOTH, LEVIATHAN, AND JOB

HEALING FROM TRAUMA IS NOT a one-time event. Imagine a person who suffered a broken leg. They were skiing down a beautiful mountain, the wind in their hair, their nose frozen from the wind chill, when suddenly . . . BAM! Broken leg. (I don't ski so I can't tell you the mechanics of the injury, but it's definitely broken.) There are going to be several steps in the healing process for that skier. There is the rescue from the ski slope, the ambulance ride to the hospital, the initial stabilization in the emergency room, maybe surgery, then weeks in a cast to allow the bone to heal, then physical therapy to regain range of motion and mobility. Each of those steps are necessary to heal the injury. Just as there can be several steps in healing from a physical injury, there can be several steps involved in healing from trauma. As trauma survivors, this metaphor of physical healing can help us identify where we are in the process. Sometimes we feel like we're in the emergency room getting treatment, sometimes we are in physical therapy, and sometimes we feel like we're still buried on the slope waiting for someone to find us and help us. Imagine how it might change our conversation as comforters if we can simply ask a survivor without judgment or expectation, "Where do you feel like you are on the journey today? Are you in the ambulance? In physical therapy? How does it feel right now?" Maybe they're fresh out of metaphorical surgery. Maybe they were heading to the hospital, but they had a setback and now it feels like the ambulance broke down and they're waiting for a tow truck. Healing can be a many-step process. Sometimes there is progress and sometimes there are setbacks, but the process is always directed toward healing.

We see this many-step process in the book of Job when it takes not one, but two divine speeches before Job can leave the ash heap of his trauma. After Job's short response in Job 40:3-5 to the first divine speech, YHWH launches into a second speech, this time centering on the much-debated Behemoth and Leviathan figures. The identities of Behemoth and Leviathan have been the subject of extensive scholarly discussion. Are they animals, perhaps a hippopotamus and a crocodile? Are they cosmic chaos monsters? Embodiments of death and evil? As with so much of the book of Job, there is not a substantial consensus on the identities of these figures.[1] One scholar's hippopotamus is another scholar's embodiment of death. What we do know is that these figures represent something enormous. In the first divine speech, God took Job on a whirlwind tour of creation showing him a plethora of animals, reveling in the beauty of creation. This second speech moves into another realm. Behemoth and Leviathan stand apart from the rest of creation, and noticeably, Job is included with them.

> Look at Behemoth,
>   which I made just as I made you. (Job 40:15)

---

[1] If you are interested in digging deeper into the different interpretations of Behemoth and Leviathan, Ortlund offers a summary of several different interpretive possibilities including: hippopotamus and crocodile; ambiguous symbols that represent the mystery of suffering; figures of Job himself; pointers to renewal of life for Job; ciphers for God; and cosmic chaos monsters (Eric Ortlund, *Piercing Levithan: God's Defeat of Evil in the Book of Job* [Downers Grove, IL: InterVarsity Press, 2021], 119-44).

There is something in these creatures that corresponds to Job's situation. And it is in this second speech that Job is able to find the resolution he needs. The big question is . . . what does Job find here?

Let's begin with a reminder that Job's most fundamental assumptions have been shattered by his experience. It is not the superficial, mundane layers of his inner schemas that have be shaken . . . like when you spend your whole life singing the wrong words to a song and suddenly one night while staring at the lyrics on the monitor during karaoke you are confronted with your mistake. No, it is Job's most fundamental, core beliefs that have been destroyed by his traumatic experience. The process of reconstructing these fundamental schemas will require something with an equally expansive size and scale. Thus, YHWH draws on figures that resonate with the most fundamental pillars of the created order. Behemoth and Leviathan, whether they are huge animals, chaos monsters, or representatives of the uncontrollable, are still figures held by God. Chaos and disorder are not running rampant, though Job's personal experience suggests otherwise. Even the chaos and disorder of Job's life is held within the hand of God. Notice this does not deny the suffering and disorder of Job's experience, just as Behemoth and Leviathan still roam free. Rather, it recognizes that even the chaos of Job's trauma is held in the hand of God. The Behemoth and Leviathan creatures demonstrate to Job that YHWH is still in control of even the most wild and chaotic creatures and circumstances.

While the exact meaning of the divine speeches is up for debate, what we can see in the text is the transformative power of the encounter. Job is changed. He is able to rebuild his world, or rather a new world is created, one that is able to hold all of Job's experiences in a way that makes sense to him. He is able to heal the open wound of his trauma and leave the ash heap. What Job finds in his encounter with YHWH in the divine speeches is a new way of understanding the world that allows for the cognitive integration of his experience and leads to the trauma resolution he needs.

Job's "Repentance"

I did warn you that we would wade into some controversial waters in our discussion of Job and trauma. This is one of those whitewater areas. Job's response to the second divine speech is one of the most hotly debated passages of Scripture. If you want to start a brawl among Hebrew Bible scholars this might be one of your go-to topics. What does Job's response to the second divine speech mean? Let's look at the text and then dive in.

> Then Job answered the LORD:
>
> "I know that you can do all things
>> and that no purpose of yours can be thwarted.
> 'Who is this that hides counsel without knowledge?'
> Therefore I have uttered what I did not understand,
>> things too wonderful for me that I did not know.
> 'Hear, and I will speak;
>> I will question you, and you declare to me.'
> I had heard of you by the hearing of the ear,
>> but now my eye sees you;
> therefore I despise myself
>> and repent in dust and ashes." (Job 42:1-6)

After the two divine speeches, after a transformative encounter with YHWH in a whirlwind, these six verses are Job's response. What in the world is he saying? After nearly forty chapters of protesting his innocence, is Job admitting guilt? Does Job really despise himself? Has Job been bullied into submission by the overwhelming power of God, and he just gives up? These verses are incredibly important to the interpretation of the text. In fact, how we interpret Job's response will have a huge impact on what we think the book of Job is all about and what we think it says about humanity, God, and suffering. There simply isn't space here to go into all of the interpretive possibilities for these verses; there are a bunch of them, they are well-researched, and I respect the many scholars who have contributed to this discussion. So, we are going to focus on what Job's response can teach us about trauma and healing.

First, I would like to offer an alternate translation of these verses. I have emphasized two thematic elements to be discussed below: knowledge and the repetition of the negative "no" or "not" phrases leading to the "but now" resolution, with the key words in italics:

And Job answered YHWH and said,

> I *know* you can do all things *and no* purpose of yours is impossible.
> "Who is this who darkens counsel without *knowledge*?"
> Surely, I spoke of what I *did not* understand, of things too wonderful that I *did not know*.
> "Hear now and I will speak. I will question you and you will make it *known*."
> I had heard of you by my ear *but now* my eye sees you.
> Therefore, I relent and am consoled for dust and ashes.[2] (Job 42:1-6, author's translation)

The first theme we see in this passage is knowledge.[3] The words *knowledge* or *to know* appear four times in these verses. This resonates with trauma as Job has been searching for reasons or explanations for what he has endured. The unknowability of his trauma is one of the sources of his struggles. He cannot explain what he cannot know, and trauma, by definition, is not immediately knowable. The emphasis on Job's lack of knowledge in these verses and the contrast with YHWH's unlimited knowledge points to a resolution of trauma that is not dependent on explanations, but instead is dependent on the integrating, or enfolding, of the trauma into a more resilient schematic framework. Job

---

[2]In addition to a trauma-theory hermeneutic, several other considerations informed this translation. First, translation choices were put in the context of a trauma narrative-type journey. Second, thematic consistency was identified. Third, poetic and lyric qualities were considered. While the challenge of bridging Hebrew and English is indeed complex and certain elements are nearly impossible to replicate, including alliteration and word patterns, this translation attempts to wed all of these considerations while maintaining fidelity to the Hebrew to present one more potential translation option.
[3]Shields likewise notes the thematic focus on knowledge in these verses (Martin Shields, "The Ignorance of Job," *Australian Biblical Review* 68 [2020]: 29).

acknowledges that he does not know the reasons for his suffering, but he is able to move toward resolution because he believes that YHWH knows.

The second important element in these verses is a poetic device centered on the repetition of the phrase *velo* translated above as "and not" or "did not." This phrase is repeated three times in Job 42:1-6. Its presence in terms of poetic lyricism culminates in Job 42:5 with the phrase *veattah* translated above as "but now." The repetitive phrasing of "and not . . . and not . . . and not . . . but now" is truly beautiful. It offers poetic resolution in terms of pattern and rhythm. This resolution in language then mirrors the cognitive resolution of Job's trauma. It is not simply poetic artistry, though that is clearly and beautifully present in the Hebrew; the phrasing also highlights Job's attempts and rejections of various failed schemas (and not . . . and not . . . and not . . .) and builds to a recognition of a new, more resilient schema with the final and determinative "but now." Not to oversimplify, but if we imagine Goldilocks in the three bears' cottage thieving their porridge and saying of each one, "and not this . . . it's too hot"; "and not this . . . it's too cold"; "but now . . . this is just right." Job had tried different explanations and none was right, until he entered into the presence of God. Job's statement that "I had heard of you by my ear, *but now* my eye sees you" dramatically illustrates this contrast. He has finally arrived at a schema that can encompass his experience and his faith. He has rebuilt his shattered window into something that will last.

Probably the stickiest verse in this passage to interpret is the final one. Job 42:6 is a challenging and controversial statement that has the power to totally change how we read the text. So, it is important that we take a bit of time to examine it, even acknowledging that the interpretation offered here is not the only possible interpretation. In the NRSVUE, the verse reads,

> Therefore I despise myself
>   and repent in dust and ashes. (Job 42:6)

I appreciate Williams's honesty when he writes, "The only translation that is not debated in 42:6 is the Hebrew construct *'al-kēn* ('therefore')."[4] Every other word in this verse is up for debate. A quick scan of various Bible translation will show how many different ways this verse has been translated, and a review of commentaries and articles will muddy the waters even further. So, with all that said, let's look at this verse from the narrow perspective of trauma and trauma resolution.

Job 42:6 contains the last words Job speaks in the text. This is his last statement on his experience, and it is the last we will hear from his perspective. This verse also contains the final words of poetry in the text. The very next verse, Job 42:7, returns to a prose form. The poetic rupture ends, and the narrative resumes. In the prose epilogue, Job is once again seen participating in familial, religious, and community roles. The return to prose suggests that the interruption or rupture of the trauma, that was represented by poetry, has been resolved and the narrative course of Job's life has resumed. Thus, the interpretive question of Job 42:6 must be held in tension with both YHWH's words and Job's actions in the epilogue. Job's reconnection with his community and his setting aside of the outward signs of his trauma response suggest that the trauma has been resolved. The poetry of Job 42:6, however, does not tell us explicitly how this was done. There is an inherent ambiguity in Job's response, and this creates fertile ground for interpretive debate.

The first issue we see in this verse is the phrase translated by the NRSVUE as "I despise myself." The problem here is the word "myself" is not in the Hebrew. In fact, there is no reflexive object for the verb *emas* translated by the NRSVUE as "despise" at all.[5] In other words, it just reads, "I despise." But despise what? Many translators have added the word "myself" in order to make the verse seem clearer, but this causes further interpretive issues. Does Job despise himself? I

---

[4]Trevor B. Williams, "Job's Unfinalizable Voice: An Addendum to David Burrell's Deconstructing Theodicy," *New Blackfriars* 101, no. 1096 (November 2020): 694.

[5]Wolfers, *Deep Things Out of Darkness*, 373.

chose to translate the verb instead as "relent."[6] Job relents in his legal case against YHWH, he relents in his complaints, he relents in his demand for answers. Job is able to set aside his yearning for an explanation and even his yearning for vindication. He relents. There must come a time in trauma processing when survivors can relent. When survivors can lay aside the need for answers, the need for justice, the need for revenge or compensation, and find healing even without any of those external contributions, as justified as those desires may be.

The next complicated word in this verse is "repent." The NRSVUE translates this part of the verse as "and repent in dust and ashes" (Job 42:6b). After spending nearly forty chapters declaring his innocence, does Job now repent? His friends have tried to pressure him into repenting to end his suffering and Job staunchly refused. He held onto his belief that his suffering was not justified; it was not the just punishment for his sins. Does he now, at the end, change his tune? So much hinges on how we read this one, single word. The Hebrew word is *nikhamtti*, which has been translated as "repent," but could also mean "comforted" or "consoled."[7] This draws attention to an important connection and literary symmetry with the beginning of the text.[8] Remember way back in Job 2, Job's friends arrived to provide comfort, something they ultimately failed to do. It is the same Hebrew root word for comfort, *nakham*, that is being used here. After the lengthy poetic middle, Job now, in this passage, finds himself ready to receive the comfort he was denied earlier. This symmetry of console and comfort echoes the symmetry of YHWH's creation language with Job's de-creation language in Job 3. The ash heap has been a locative symbol for Job's experience of trauma. When he is finally given, and can accept, comfort for his losses, he is able to rise from the ash heap and return to his community.

---

[6]See David J. A. Clines, *Job 38–42* (Grand Rapids, MI: HarperCollins Christian, 2015), 1207-10 for a helpful discussion on the etymology of the verb and his connection of *emas* with the legal metaphor. See also Eugene Merrill, "מאס," *NIDOTTE*, 2:833 for a lexical analysis.

[7]Clines, *Job 38–42*, 1220.

[8]Clines, *Job 38–42*, 461.

Ultimately, the meaning and translation of this key verse is far from settled. The Hebrew itself allows for the legitimacy of several different translations. The fact that so many wildly different translations can be supported by the Hebrew text adds fuel to the interpretive fire concerning Job's second response. Given the nature of poetry itself and the literary artistry of the book of Job, it is possible that the author intended to leave this verse ambiguous and open to debate. It is, perhaps, not unlike the concluding stanza of Robert Frost's poem "The Road Not Taken."[9]

> I shall be telling this with a sigh
> Somewhere ages and ages hence:
> Two roads diverged in a wood, and I—
> I took the one less traveled by,
> And that has made all the difference.

For some readers, the meaning of these iconic closing lines may seem obvious. The poet chose the less traveled road, and lived happily ever after. However, the poem does not say that. It is equally possible that choosing the less traveled road had a negative impact on the poet and in ages hence he will sigh out of regret. Both interpretations are valid and legitimate readings of the poem. The intentional ambiguity and interpretive freedom are part of what makes the poem so compelling. Perhaps, the Joban poet was exercising similar artistry in this verse allowing the multiple potential meanings to confront and complement each other.

When we look at this verse with an eye for what it can teach us about trauma, one of the primary things we will notice is that we have to become comfortable with ambiguity. Trauma is messy and there won't always be a clear-cut path forward to healing. Sometimes what resonates with a trauma survivor may not make sense to us. There may be breakthroughs and glimmers of awareness that, as comforters, we don't

---

[9] Robert Frost, *Selected Poems* (New York: Fall River Press, 2011), 153.

understand. A survivor may not even be able to articulate the step that takes them to resolution. Trauma can be many things all at once, just as this verse can mean many things all at once. This ambiguity runs counter to much of what we have been taught: that there is only one right answer, that the path forward is always clear. When coming alongside a trauma survivor, comforters have be okay with ambiguity. Some things may never make sense, but the goal is not an explanation, the goal is resolution. Job did not have just one failed schema that needed to be rebuilt, but an entire conceptual hierarchy to be reconstructed. Job was rebuilding his schemas from the foundation up. So, while one clear-cut translation and interpretation of this verse would be attractive for biblical interpreters, the ambiguity and multiple layers of meaning contained within this verse illustrate the complex nature of trauma resolution. For trauma survivors, multiple things can be true at the same time. This holds true for the healing process as well. As with poetry itself, one thing for a survivor can point to many things. Instead of pressuring survivors for an answer, we should be walking with them to healing.

Rebuilding in the Church

All of this sounds well and good, but how do we apply it? The chances of God appearing in a whirlwind while we are sitting with a trauma survivor, or when we are the trauma survivor, are slim (though always possible). In a world and more specifically in churches that are becoming more aware of and sensitive to mental health issues and trauma, approaching the book of Job from a trauma-informed perspective has the potential to significantly impact how churches, pastors, scholars, and lay believers minister to people suffering from trauma and trauma responses. It shows us the failure of rehearsed theological answers in the face of individual trauma. Job's friends may be effective, if misguided, theologians, but they fail as comforters and trusted listeners. Such an understanding of the friends' missteps serves as a cautionary tale in how comforters counsel and support trauma survivors.

The book of Job warns us against trying to impose a collective story or explanation on an experience of individual trauma. This is seen in Job's resistance to his friends' explanations of his suffering and their calls for his repentance. It is also seen in the lack of explanation given in the divine speeches. The book of Job testifies to the importance of honoring individual suffering and the voice of the trauma survivor. The means of resolution for the survivor may not make sense or offer a clear explanation from a systematic theology standpoint, but the more important issue is how the means of resolution functioned for the survivor. This emphasis challenges pastors and church leaders to listen, really listen, to the voices of survivors and empower them to rebuild their shattered window in their own individual way.

LESSONS LEARNED

- Healing from trauma is a many-step process. Sometimes there is forward progress, sometimes we take a step back.

- In trauma healing, multiple things can be true at the same time. As survivors and comforters, we may have to become comfortable with ambiguity.

- There are many different ways to translate Job's response in Job 42:6. Each translation will impact how we view the text and what we think the text means.

REFLECTION QUESTIONS

- What do you think Job means with his final words in Job 42:6? Do you think Job repents? Do you think he is comforted? How does this impact your view of the book of Job as a whole?

- How comfortable are you with ambiguity? How strong is your need for answers and explanations for life's circumstances?

- Where are you in your own healing journey today?

NINE

PUTTING A SHATTERED WORLD BACK TOGETHER

I HAVE LONG BEEN FASCINATED with the Japanese art of *kintsugi*. I first heard about it when a sexual assault survivor shared her story and used the idea of *kintsugi* as an illustration of her healing journey. In *kintsugi*, broken pieces of ceramic or pottery are repaired using gold. Imagine a vase or a bowl that has been dropped and has broken into pieces. For many of us, our instinct would be to sweep it up and toss the whole thing in the trash. We might be a little sad to lose something we cared about, but looking at the destruction and the shattered pieces, it seems broken beyond repair, worthless, no longer of value. So, we throw it away. As a survivor, I know how it feels to be pushed aside, to be seen as broken beyond repair, and no longer of value—to look into the eyes of people you trusted as they throw you away. There is no doubt that trauma is a shattering. Things can never go back to the way they were before. Life has changed. But that doesn't mean life is over.

Now let's imagine a different outcome. Instead of tossing the broken bowl away, let's carefully gather up the broken pieces. We fit them back together and fill the seams with gold. Not glue, not puddy, not spackle.

Gold. Precious, beautiful, gold. We fit each piece to another, rebuilding what was broken and letting the gold scars shine through. Now, this bowl that seemed lost and useless is more valuable than it was before. It is the scars that make it precious. Those gold scars don't hide where the pain hit, they don't cover up what was broken, instead the scars make it more beautiful. We can point to a vein of gold and say, "See there, right there is where it was broken, but with time and care it is stronger and more beautiful than before." What was once a bowl or a vase or a plate is now a work of art. And the beauty is in the scars.

After his final poetic words in Job 42:6, Job leaves the ash heap and rejoins his community, but he carries the scars with him. As the poetic rupture of trauma is resolved and the narrative continues, Job is changed. Life does not go back to the way it was before, but life does go on. The shift in genre from poetry back to prose in Job 42:7 illustrates the shift in his trauma healing. Whatever it was that Job understood in the divine speeches, he received what he needed to integrate the traumatic experience and file it away. It is no longer a collection of fragments with sharp edges that intrude and shake him. Job is able to take the experience and enfold it into his life story. He is now free to look at the experience when he chooses and not be overtaken by flashbacks or intrusive thoughts. Job has found a way to express his experience and has found meaning in it, even if that meaning is never explicitly explained. His final words in Job 42:6 are the last touches on his rebuilt window. Now, in the closing verses of the text, Job rises from the dust and ashes and steps back into his community. These closing verses not only illustrate Job's healing, but they teach us, as the church, so much about trauma healing.

The epilogue in Job 42:7-17 returns us to the narrator, who details YHWH's rebuke of Job's friends, Job's restoration, and provides a wrap-up of the rest of Job's life. There are four specific elements of the epilogue that I want to look at: (1) YHWH's commendation of Job's words and his rebuke of the friends; (2) Job's intercession for his friends and his twofold restoration; (3) the role of the community in Job's resolution; and (4) the reference to Job's daughters. Each of these elements reflects a way in which a survivor's community can actively support healing. The role of the community in Job's healing is quite powerful. Job, who has been isolated and alone in the ash heap, is once again embraced by his community, and it is in the presence of the community that we see Job restored. As we will see in this section, it is a mistake to think that the community does not have an impact on a trauma survivor's healing. The community can support and care for a survivor or, like Job's friends, a community, even a Christian community, can inflict additional wounding and pain. Are we instruments of gold helping repair the shattered parts? Or are we janitors sweeping away the broken pieces that no longer benefit us?

RECOGNITION AND RESTITUTION

Trauma expert Judith Herman suggests there are two specific things a trauma survivor needs from their community in order for the survivor to embrace a renewed sense of meaning in the world: recognition and restitution. Herman writes,

> The response of the community has a powerful influence on the ultimate resolution of the trauma. Restoration of the breach between the traumatized person and the community depends, first, on public acknowledgment of the traumatic event and, second, on some form of community action. Once it is publicly recognized that a person has been harmed, the community must take action to assign responsibility for the harm and to repair the injury. These two responses—recognition and restitution—are necessary to rebuild the survivor's sense of order and justice.[1]

The first community response Herman suggests is recognition. Survivors need their experience to be recognized. Now, it may not be

---

[1]Judith Herman, *Trauma and Recovery: The Aftermath of Violence—from Domestic Abuse to Political Terror* (New York: Basic Books), 70.

in neon lights or announced in a church newsletter, but the trauma needs to be brought into the light. Survivors need to hear that what happened to them was wrong. Our tendency, however, is to ignore, cover up, or hide the ugly business of trauma. Once we get a survivor to a place of forgiveness, or at least a place of coping well, we often push the traumatic event into the dark recesses of history, never to be spoken of again. This does a disservice to trauma survivors. It is important that, as comforters, we recognize and honor the bad as well as the good. Survivors need to know that their experience did not happen in a vacuum, that it has not been forgotten or stuffed in a drawer. There is empowerment and healing when we intentionally make space to talk about terrible things.

Too often churches have shied away from discussing trauma. There can be lots of reasons for this hesitancy. Trauma can make us afraid. Trauma can make us uncomfortable. Trauma can shatter our own beliefs and assumptions about the world or about people we trust. In cases of abuse within institutions likes churches, schools, businesses, or youth activities, we can be shaken to our core. Some witnesses may immediately try to cover it up or defend an abusive leader because to accept that the accusations might be true would be overwhelming . . . it would shatter their window. Some witnesses may lose their sense of safety and trust in the community if they acknowledge what has occurred. It can all get messy and frightening. But if we don't talk about it honestly, if we aren't willing to face the shadows, the darkness will only grow.

Sometimes, in churches, it is as if we are afraid to acknowledge the difficulties, tragedies, and horrors of life. We want to focus on the shiny, the good, and the triumphant. Isn't that why so often we restrict a "testimony" to a story that has a happy ending? But a testimony shouldn't just be when things work out the way we want. Sometimes the true testimony is when things went wrong and stayed wrong, yet a survivor survived. If we only talk about and share the stories of good news, the cancer that disappeared, the marriage that was restored, the forgiveness and reconciliation, then we are not only intentionally disregarding the tragedies, but we are also sending a message that the only stories that are worth sharing are the ones where everyone lives happily ever after. If we idolize redemption stories and happy endings, people who are still healing may remain silent, thinking they haven't made it yet, and the church will miss out on the beauty, lessons, and faithfulness that are present in the pain. Let me say it again: God met Job in the ashes. That is a testimony that is worth sharing. We need to show people, both believers and unbelievers, that the church is not just a place of triumph and praise, but a place where lament, mourning, crying, suffering, and anger are welcomed and allowed to be expressed.

So, there needs to be a recognition of the traumatic event. Not necessarily a big public announcement, it doesn't have to be posted on social media, but someone from the community, a pastor, a church leader, a friend, needs to be able to look the survivor in the eye and say, "This was a terrible thing, it wasn't right, and it should not have happened to you." Imagine the difference that simple statement could make to someone who feels alone, unseen, and unheard. It gives survivors permission to share their story, all of their story, and show them that they are still loved, sharp edges and all. If you are a trauma survivor, I want you to hear this from me. "What you went through was terrible. It wasn't right, and it should not have happened to you. You survived and you are healing. That is an incredible testimony, and I am so proud of you."[2]

We see an example of this type of recognition in the epilogue:

After the LORD had spoken these words to Job, the LORD said to Eliphaz the Temanite: "My wrath is kindled against you and against your two friends, for you have not spoken of me what is right, as my servant Job has." (Job 42:7)

---

[2]If you need someone to talk to about what you have been through, please consider contacting a mental health professional with experience in trauma. You deserve to heal.

In this verse, YHWH recognizes Job's right speech and rebukes the friends' wrong speech. There is debate, of course, about what exactly in Job's speech is being commended. After all, Job did say some pretty shocking things, but what cannot be denied is that Job is commended by YHWH and the friends are rebuked. From the very beginning of the book of Job, the issue of Job's speech had been the subject of debate. This whole thing started when *hassatan* suggested Job would curse God in his suffering. Later on, Job's friends repeatedly criticized the words Job spoke. However, here, at the end of the text, Job is commended by YHWH for speaking rightly. Why? J. Richard Middleton suggests an important translation distinction in this verse. He suggests that the better translation of the Hebrew preposition *el* is "to" rather than "about."[3] This would mean that Job had been right in speaking *to* God where the friends only spoke *about* God.[4] In this case, the emphasis would be on the relationship between Job and YHWH.[5] Speaking "to" implies relationship, while speaking "about" implies explanation.[6] It seems that Job was right in speaking *to* God in voicing his protests and expressing his yearning for a face-to-face encounter and that act of speaking to God is being commended, without forgetting the correction, or teaching, that YHWH also brought to Job.

In addition to commending Job's speech, YHWH refers to Job as "my servant" four times in this passage:

> After the LORD had spoken these words to Job, the LORD said to
> Eliphaz the Temanite: "My wrath is kindled against you and against

---

[3]J. Richard Middleton, *Abraham's Silence: The Binding of Isaac, the Suffering of Job, and How to Talk Back to God* (Grand Rapids, MI: Baker Academic, 2021), 126. Janzen argues the same point, highlighting the predominance of *'el* as indicating to whom the subject is speaking (J. Gerald Janzen, *At the Scent of Water: The Ground of Hope in the Book of Job* [Grand Rapids, MI: Eerdmans, 2009], 106).

[4]Middleton, *Abraham's Silence*, 126.

[5]Choon-Leong Seow, *Job 1–21: Interpretation and Commentary* (Grand Rapids, MI: Eerdmans, 2013), 92.

[6]Seow, *Job 1–21*, 92.

your two friends, for you have not spoken of me what is right, as *my servant Job* has. Now therefore take seven bulls and seven rams, and go to *my servant Job*, and offer up for yourselves a burnt offering, and *my servant Job* shall pray for you, for I will accept his prayer not to deal with you according to your folly, for you have not spoken of me what is right, as *my servant Job* has done." (Job 42:7-8, emphasis added).

This reference to Job as "my servant" recalls YHWH's characterization of Job in the prologue. There YHWH refers to Job as "my servant Job" twice. YHWH's characterization of Job as a servant involves being blameless, upright, fearing God, and turning away from evil (see Job 2:8). Interestingly, in the epilogue, Job is referred to as a servant of YHWH four times, double the number of references in the prologue. The repeated use of this phrase in the epilogue demonstrates that Job remains a servant of YHWH. He is singled out in the epilogue as blameless, upright, fearing God, and turning from evil. Job is vindicated before the friends who accused him of sin, and he is vindicated in front of the community that isolated him. This vindication functions as a type of recognition. YHWH recognizes that Job was treated wrongly.

The second element Herman notes is restitution. Restitution is closely connected to justice. What we see in the epilogue is an intentional act of restitution.

And the LORD restored the fortunes of Job when he had prayed for his friends, and the LORD gave Job twice as much as he had before. (Job 42:10)

Job receives back double what he had lost. This verse makes it explicit that it is the Lord who is providing the double recompense. Job's fortunes are not merely restored, they are doubled. This is significant because it seems to refer to the recompense required for theft in Exodus: "When the animal, whether ox or donkey or sheep, is found alive in the thief's possession, the thief shall pay double" (Ex 22:4). Clines suggests this double recompense in the epilogue is an admission by YHWH of his responsibility for the wrongs done to Job.[7] It is understandably challenging for many of us to consider that God may be accepting responsibility for Job's suffering. It is a theological conundrum . . . is God really admitting to inflicting unjust suffering on a righteous man? However, from the perspective of trauma theory, such an assertion can be explained by the need of the survivor for recognition and restitution. In acknowledging Job's mistreatment at the hands of YHWH, as theologically difficult as that might be for some readers, the epilogue narrative provides Job with a way to assign responsibility for his suffering. YHWH has already acknowledged his role in Job's suffering in Job 2:3b when he says to *hassatan* "you incited me against him, to destroy him for no reason." Thus, the epilogue is not suggesting something that has not been stipulated from the beginning. What the epilogue does do is make that connection clear to Job. This double recompense thus functions as both recognition and restitution.

Unfortunately, there are many trauma survivors who will never receive recognition or restitution from the perpetrator of their wounding. A natural disaster has no one to speak for it. Some abusers have died, some simply refuse to take responsibility for their actions, some are unsafe to be around and engage with. This lack of recognition and restitution from the perpetrator may be a hard reality for a survivor to accept. If we think back to playgrounds and playdates, when someone hurts us, they are supposed to apologize. They might be forced to apologize by their parent, but the fact remains . . . harms require amends. It is hardwired into us as children. But that hardwiring often fizzles out in the reality of adulthood. Pride, self-interest, legalities, litigation, reputation, platform, prestige, paychecks, any number of

---

[7]David J. A. Clines, *Job 38–42* (Grand Rapids, MI: HarperCollins Christian, 2015), 1237. Balentine adds, "It is hard to overlook the connection elsewhere in the Old Testament between double compensation and (at least) a tacit admission of guilt" (Samuel Balentine, *Job* [Macon, GA: Smyth & Helwys, 2006], 715).

these and more can play into a someone who commits harm being unwilling to acknowledge and apologize for their actions.

Just as with the need for recognition, the community can step in and help a survivor with restitution as well. The survivor might never receive an apology or amends from the perpetrator, but the community can stand in and assist the survivor. It might be something as simple as "I'm sorry this happened to you." Or there may be practical needs stemming from the trauma that the community can help meet. If restitution is an act of attempting to make a wounded person whole again, that restitution, which is owed by the perpetrator, can be facilitated by the survivor's support system. Never underestimate the blessing of meeting a need.

RESTORATION

Trauma strips us of our sense of control and power. Survivors, who had no control over the trauma-inducing event and who have not had advocates or comforters respond to their story, may stop believing that they have any control or any meaningful agency in the world.[8] So, one step in trauma healing can be a recovered sense of personal agency. From this perspective, the epilogue in the book of Job gives us several examples of ways that Job's meaningful agency in the world is restored.

First, Job is restored to his priestly role. Now, we have to pause here a moment and address the priestly elephant in the room. The story of Job is set outside of Israel and there is no mention in the text of the Levitical priesthood. So, Job was most likely not an official priest. However, what we see in the book of Job from the very beginning is how Job acts in a priestly-type role with religious responsibility and authority. When we are first introduced to Job, we learn that he offers sacrifices on behalf of his children.[9] Then here, in the epilogue,

---

[8]Serene Jones, *Trauma and Grace: Theology in a Ruptured World* (Louisville, KY: Westminster John Knox, 2019), 17.
[9]Balentine, *Job*, 711.

YHWH tells the friends to go to Job and ask him to intercede on their behalf:

> Now therefore take seven bulls and seven rams, and go to my servant
> Job, and offer up for yourselves a burnt offering, and my servant Job
> shall pray for you, for I will accept his prayer not to deal with you ac-
> cording to your folly, for you have not spoken of me what is right, as
> my servant Job has done. (Job 42:8)

It is YHWH himself who restores Job to an effective religious role. The friends, who had been so convinced of their own piety and right-eousness in the dialogues, are told they must go to the very man they accused of terrible sins and ask for his help in order for them to be for-given. Job is restored to his intercessory role and told it will be effective for turning away YHWH's wrath. In this act, Job is given an opportunity to act with impactful and meaningful personal agency. A sense of purpose and control is returned to him. The world that he had felt was disordered, chaotic, and dangerous has been reordered in the divine speeches and Job is invited to participate in that right order once again. Job is shown that his actions can have a positive effect on the world.[10]

And let's notice here that Job's intercession for his friends comes before any of his fortunes are restored. His friends come to him and ask him to intercede for them with YHWH and Job agrees. He agrees to pray for the people who had condemned and wounded him. This takes us back to the initial challenge raised by *hassatan* in the prologue. Job's intercession comes with no promise of restoration or wealth. He acts because YHWH asked it of him, with no promise of benefit. Before any hint of the coming restitution, YHWH first restores Job to his religious role. His calling and purpose, which were never removed by God, have been publicly restored to him. Job's friends, who have loudly and repeatedly accused him of sin, are forced to turn to him for prayer to prevent YHWH from "dealing with you according to your

---

[10]Jones, *Trauma and Grace*, 93.

folly" (Job 42:7). The very people who were Job's most vocal accusers must now tell Job they need his intercession with God.

Next, Job is restored to his community. The first step in Job's restoration to the community is his intercession for his friends.[11] Following this act, YHWH provides a double recompense to Job, and then the community that had isolated Job returns to him.

> Then there came to him all his brothers and sisters and all who had known him before, and they ate bread with him in his house; they showed him sympathy and comforted him for all the evil that the LORD had brought upon him; and each of them gave him a piece of money and a gold ring. (Job 42:11)

Job is embraced as a trauma survivor. The table fellowship implies restored relationships. While the prologue does not specifically mention abandonment by his extended family, the implication, based on Job's location on the ash heap and the social separation his skin disease probably required, is there. Further, the words of his wife in Job 2:9 speak to a tone of rejection by his loved ones. As we have learned, trauma often results in alienation and isolation, both of which Job experienced. He was isolated from his community on the ash heap and alienated from his wife and his friends by their inability to act as trusted listeners. The words "they showed him sympathy and comforted him for all the evil that the LORD had brought upon him" implies an acceptance of Job's story, all of his story, including the trauma. Job's trauma story becomes a testimony as it is heard and embraced by the community. He is restored to his community with the truth of his experience intact. His community comes to him now as the comforters that the friends failed to be.

If we go back to the when the friends first arrived on the scene, we see that they came to "console and comfort him" (Job 2:11b). They failed. Miserably. They end up rebuked by God for the things they said

---

[11]Kathleen O'Connor, *Job* (Collegeville, MN: Liturgical Press, 2012), 99.

to Job. Let that be a lesson to us. God watches the way we treat the hurting. God sees and God knows. All of our fancy buildings and budgets and business decisions won't count for anything if we had to step on a wounded brother or sister to get there. How we treat the wounded in our midst is a testimony to how we view God. Job's friends thought they had all the answers. They thought they knew exactly what God wanted. They stepped all over Job to prove that they were right. And, in the end, they are rebuked by God for it. From the depths of the whirlwind, they hear "you got it wrong."

That should be a stern warning to all of us in leadership. God's priority is people. It's not a new building or a new team or a bigger platform. It's people. If we leave Job for a moment and skip forward to the New Testament, we see this in vivid detail. Jesus did not turn away the hurting and the wounded. He reached out to the sick, the sinner, and the lost. He touched them, embraced them, and loved them. When Job was alone in his suffering and condemned by his friends, God showed up. That is the legacy of the whirlwind. We meet people in their pain and walk with them through the ashes. Job's community comes to him and embraces him. They embrace his story. They embrace his transformation. That is the power of community.

Job's restoration to his community is also seen in another small detail in the epilogue that is easy to miss.

> The LORD blessed the latter days of Job more than his beginning, and he had fourteen thousand sheep, six thousand camels, a thousand yoke of oxen, and a thousand donkeys. He also had seven sons and three daughters. He named the first Jemimah, the second Keziah, and the third Keren-happuch. In all the land there were no women so beautiful as Job's daughters, and their father gave them an inheritance along with their brothers. (Job 42:12-15)

Right in the middle of listing all of Job's fortunes, the author notes the names of Job's daughters. What an odd thing to mention. And not only do we get their names, but the author tells us that Job gave each of them an inheritance along with his sons. Why is this in the text? What do Job's daughters have to do with anything? One interesting suggestion from the perspective of trauma healing is that it suggests a reconnection with future generations. In order to connect with the next generation, we must have a sense of meaning, hope, and continuance in life. Trauma distorts all of these. "Connecting with the next generation means the person who experienced the traumatic event has healed enough to acknowledge that life continues."[12] Additionally, the fact that the text specifically names Job's daughters and states that Job grants them inheritances leads to speculation about the impact Job's trauma has had on him.

The inclusion of the names of Job's daughters and his provision for them is a powerful evolution from the prologue. In Job 1, the daughters are unnamed and Job's acts on their behalf involve sacrifices that appear to be attempts to protect them from tragedy. He offers sacrifices for his children as a "just in case" type of act. Sadly, this attempt at protection fails and his children die. In the epilogue, however, Job both names and provides for his daughters. Job has indeed been restored to his community, but in a different manner. Ortlund sees in this detail evidence of Job's expanded understanding of God and the working of the world:

> Without any outside prompting, however, Job sets aside funds for his three daughters in case they are widowed. This small detail reveals how profoundly Job has been reconciled to God's present administration of creation, in which the normal order of things is safety and blessing, but not every tragedy is prevented ahead of time. Job, knowing his own daughters may suffer widowhood, has turned from protesting against a God who would allow such things to doing what he can to care for those who may suffer.[13]

---

[12]Caralie Focht, "The Joseph Story: A Trauma-Informed Biblical Hermeneutic for Pastoral Care Providers," *Pastoral Psychology* 69, no. 3 (June 2020): 221.

[13]Eric Ortlund, *Piercing Leviathan: God's Defeat of Evil in the Book of Job* (Downers Grove, IL: InterVarsity Press, 2021), 171.

Job has been changed. Though he has reconnected with his community, his experience of trauma and his encounter with YHWH have changed him, and those changes are being lived out. Job has changed the way he interacts with his children. He recognizes the vulnerability of life and does something about it. Job takes the lessons he has learned and the way his experience has shaped him and gives those lessons legs.

Some trauma survivors may choose to take their own experience of trauma and turn it into something positive, something that can impact others, protect others, or serve others. This is one more way survivors may choose to make meaning and find purpose in a horrific experience. Someone who suffers sexual assault may become a voice for other survivors. Someone who is injured in a drunk driving accident may advocate for legal changes. Not every survivor will want to take this route and that is okay; there shouldn't be any pressure on a survivor to speak about or share their experience. Trauma changes us, but it is not our identity. It is simply one part of our story. We are first and foremost image bearers of God. Trauma cannot change that.

The naming of Job's daughters and their inheritances are signs that trauma leaves us different than before. There is no going back to how things were. We have seen too much, we know too much, we have walked through too much to go back to the life we had before. The book of Job shows us that even with his fortunes restored, even with his restoration as a priestly-type authority, even with his community embracing him and supporting him, Job is scarred. His first ten children are still dead. The wounding and horror of the ash heap cannot be undone. Job's shattered window has been repaired but there are scars. The beauty in the story, the beauty in all our stories of wounding and suffering, is that those scars can be filled with gold.

Lessons Learned

- Many trauma survivors long for recognition and restitution. Recognition acknowledges the wrong that was done, and restitution attempts to make amends. When the perpetrator cannot or will not provide these, the community can step in and offer support to the survivor.

- Trauma often causes survivors to be isolated and alienated from their community. In Job's restoration he is restored to his priestly-type role and embraced by his community as a trauma survivor.

- The naming of Job's daughters and their inheritances illustrates that trauma changes us and changes how we view the world.

Reflection Questions

- What does Job's receiving a double recompense from God mean for you? Does this challenge the way you think of God or of suffering?

- Is there an area of justice, advocacy, or support that you have been inspired to work in because of your own experiences? What would that look like for you?

- Looking back over the totality of the book of Job, what stands out to you? Has your perspective on the book changed at all? How would you explain the book of Job to others?

TEN

....

A CHURCH OF DUST
AND ASHES

TO BE HUMAN IS TO BE VULNERABLE. I'm sure there aren't many of us who love that idea. We are not invincible, impervious, unbreakable beings. We are dust and ashes, fragile creatures in a broken world, and sometimes we find ourselves in pieces. There is a beautiful connection in Job's final words that speaks to this vulnerable reality of humanity. The reference in this line to "dust and ashes" recalls Abraham's words in Genesis when he negotiates with the Lord for the people of Sodom and Gomorrah:

> Abraham answered, "Let me take it upon myself to speak to my lord, I who am but dust and ashes." (Gen 18:27)

In this interpretation, Job's use of the phrase "dust and ashes" becomes a statement on the human condition.[1] We were formed from the dust and to the dust we will return. We are created creatures and as such we may suffer the slings and arrows of this world, a world marred by sin, a world yearning for the new creation.

---

[1]Tina Pippin, "Job 42:1-6, 10-17," *Interpretation* 53, no. 3 (July 1999): 299.

While there is plenty of room for debate about what exactly Job meant by the phrase "dust and ashes," it is worthwhile for our discussion to look for a moment at the reality of our humanity, a humanity that is lived in community. Our churches are made up of people formed from the dust of the earth. There are no perfect people, and our imperfections will bump up against one another. We live in community, sometimes several different types of communities, but none of us an island. The church community is meant to be a place of healing, restoration, and comfort. A place where we worship together, serve together, and grow together. Unfortunately, as we have seen in the book of Job, sometimes the community that is meant to be our safest place becomes a place of wounding instead. No one likes to admit it, but we cannot change what we cannot acknowledge.

The purpose of this book and this journey we have taken through the book of Job is to learn how to become better stewards of other people's pain. How do we come alongside someone who is walking through trauma in a way that promotes healing and does not inflict further pain? How do we avoid being "miserable comforters" and instead become a community of comforters that cares for, supports, and consoles the wounded? How can we be trusted listeners who sit in the ashes with the hurting and remind them that they are not alone? The harsh realities of recent years have turned our eyes to the hidden pain and burdens that many of our brothers and sisters have been carrying. The COVID-19 pandemic, abuse, betrayal, racism, NDAs, MeToo, ChurchToo, dark things are coming to light and the church needs to play a role in bandaging these wounds and walking with survivors. If we fail in ministering to the wounded, we shouldn't be surprised when we lose the trust of those who witness it.

BRINGING IT ALL TOGETHER

This is the part where we take all the threads we have been pulling, all the paths we have been following, and bring them together. How do we make all this information practical and applicable for the life of the church? Theory is great and necessary, but practice is where the academic rubber meets the road. So, let's look at some concrete steps pastors, church leaders, and believers can take to minister to trauma survivors in a healthy and healing way. As a framework, I am going to suggest three things we, as comforters, can provide a trauma survivor: a place of sanctuary, a place to tell their story, and a place to belong. These three ideas are based on Judith Herman's three stages of healing: safety, remembrance and mourning, and reconnection to community.[2]

A word of caution before we jump in: we should not approach these three stages as a clearly defined, linear progression with milestones to be checked off as a survivor sprints toward healing. Instead, these are broad categories that encompass the general needs a survivor may have to resolve their trauma. In reality, the process will probably look more like a tangle of Christmas lights than a straight line. There will be ups and downs, good days and bad days, two steps forward and two steps back, there will be repetition and intrusive thoughts, and all of that is okay. As pastors, church leaders, believers, and friends we can work to provide a sanctuary of safety for a survivor, we can listen to their story, and we can give them a place, whether that is a community or a friendship, where they belong and they know they are accepted, loved, and embraced.

I say all of this up front because choosing to come alongside a trauma survivor is not a decision to be made lightly. We are dealing with people whose worlds have been tossed upside down. Their windows are broken, and their hearts are bleeding. This is not a "let's meet once or twice for coffee and get you back on the horse" kind of commitment. There is nothing wrong with recognizing our limitations. At any given moment all of us will be in a place where this kind

---

[2]Judith Herman, *Trauma and Recovery: The Aftermath of Violence—from Domestic Abuse to Political Terror* (New York: Basic Books).

of friendship, support, and care is simply beyond us. There are lots of good reasons for not being able to be the one to walk beside a trauma survivor during their healing journey. It is far better to recognize it early than jump in and have to bail halfway through. Knowing your limitations is a sign of maturity. Only the immature take on a task simply because it's there. So, take the time to pray about whether you are the right person at the right time for this journey, and even if you are not, you can still commit to praying for the survivor. Mountains are moved and breakthroughs happen in prayer. There may also be other ways you can offer support and encouragement: maybe bringing a meal or sending a gift card, helping with yard work, babysitting, filling in on a volunteer team. Just as we should not underestimate the blessing of just being present, we shouldn't underestimate the blessing of meeting someone's everyday needs.

A PLACE OF SANCTUARY

It's hard to prepare for a storm when you're in one. And it's hard to heal from trauma when the trauma-inducing situation is still happening. It's kind of like those cartoons where there is a hole in a boat and as the boat sinks the characters frantically try to bail out the water but the hole in the boat just keeps letting more water in. You have to plug the hole before you can deal with the water that's already in the boat. Trauma processing is a bit like that. It will be difficult, if not impossible, for a survivor to begin working through their trauma if they are still in a trauma-inducing situation. As a trusted witness for a trauma survivor, we can provide a place of sanctuary that is safe, healthy, and supportive.

Safety comes in different forms. The first is physical safety. Are they safe from harm being inflicted by others and harm they may cause themselves? Are their basic needs being met? Do they have shelter, food, and any necessary medical care? We shouldn't overlook these simple questions. It will be difficult to help a spouse recover from the trauma of domestic violence if they will leave a meeting and go home only to be abused again. It will be difficult to help a survivor of a traumatic accident or medical diagnosis if they cannot get the treatment they need. It will be difficult to help a survivor of childhood sexual abuse deal with their trauma response if they are actively suicidal. The issue of physical safety should be one of the first questions we ask a survivor who has come to us for help. It can be as simple as the following:

"Are you safe in your home?"
"Are you in danger of being hurt by someone?"
"Are you planning to harm yourself?"
"Do you have a safe place to stay?"

This concern for their physical well-being is not just responsible, it demonstrates your care for them as a person. It shows that you have seen their unique situation and you want to know about it.

Safety also encompasses emotional and spiritual safety. Pastors, church leaders, and mature believers can have a great deal of influence over the people they mentor, lead, and counsel. It is our responsibility as trusted leaders to establish a sanctuary where the survivor will be free from emotional manipulation, coercion, and abuse. This includes the way we welcome or exclude a survivor from our community. In order for survivors to feel safe and welcome in our churches, we have to intentionally create an environment where suffering is allowed. If we always put the happy people up front, if we only preach about the victory and benefits of Christianity, if we tell people that if they pray enough and give enough and have enough faith nothing but blessings will come their way, we turn what should be a sanctuary for the hurting into a show for the powerful. If we never tell people that it's okay to cry, to yell, and to question, then we are creating an environment where suffering is seen as failure. It creates unrealistic expectations and allows shame to take hold. If survivors hear the message, spoken or unspoken, that suffering is a sign of sin, doubt is failure, and tears show a lack of faith, then we are not only being dishonest, but we are also not so subtly excluding the wounded from our midst. Come back when you've figured it out, come back when you're healed, come back when you've got a happy ending to share. Come back when you're not so messy. A true place of sanctuary is open to the messy, the hurting, and the wounded. After all, it is not the happy and perfect who need to find refuge, but those who are in desperate need of help.

As I said in the beginning, the trauma response is not something to be ashamed of. We are fearfully and wonderfully made with a trauma response that functions to help us survive. If a survivor has lived through trauma, then they should be celebrated. Their trauma response did exactly what it was supposed to do. That trauma response might need some help resetting now, but that is not a sign that the survivor is broken. If we attach shame to trauma, we are inflicting a secondary injury on someone who is already hurting. So, establishing physical safety as well as an emotionally and spiritually safe place for the survivor to tell their story is the first step in walking with a survivor.

What Does a Place of Sanctuary Look Like?

- Ask a survivor about their situation and safety. Avoiding the uncomfortable questions does not make them go away. The more we can address the tough issues with compassion and love, the more we help a survivor find safety and establish ourselves as trustworthy persons.

- Be intentional about creating a space where a survivor can feel secure. Trust is a casualty of trauma, and a survivor may have lost trust not only in their perpetrator, but in the world in general, and that may include those of us who are trying to help. Establishing trust with a survivor will take time and intentionality.

- Trust and safety include guarding the survivor's story. Sharing their story without permission, even with the best of intentions, is a violation of trust. Ask the survivor for permission before you share their story with anyone. "I'd like to have the prayer team praying for you. May I tell them what you have been through?" Be specific about what you will be sharing and respect their choice if they say no. A survivor being taken by surprise because someone else knows their story will further shake their sense of safety and increase feelings of vulnerability. If something has occurred that as a mandated reporter you are required to report, tell the survivor what you are going to do and why.

- Be willing and be prepared to share outside resources with a survivor in need. This may mean cultivating connections in your city or community before trauma strikes so you have a list of resources, care givers, and professionals you can reach out to when needed.

- Fight for the survivor. Many trauma survivors feel abandoned, alone, and helpless in the face of a trauma-inducing event. Standing with the survivor and being with them, both literally and metaphorically, can help create a feeling of safety and trust. They will know someone is beside them and willing to fight for them. This may mean something as simple as sitting with them in church so they are not alone or talking with them after church so they feel welcomed and loved. Shame can be a powerful influence on survivors and having a friend by their side can help overcome or mitigate feelings of shame.

- Pray for the survivor. A sanctuary doesn't just mean a place of safety, it can also mean a place of worship and prayer. We can pray for the wounded and hurting even if they never hear a single word of it. As we pray for healing and restoration, we can trust that God hears, God sees, and God is at work.

A Place to Tell Their Story

Herman's second stage of healing is remembrance and mourning. This stage involves not only piecing together the fragmented and jagged memories of the trauma-inducing event, but also mourning and grieving for what was lost. It is in this stage that a survivor begins to tell their story. As comforters we can provide a place where survivors can tell their story without fear. As we discussed earlier, their story will probably not start out as a coherent narrative with a neat beginning, middle, and end. The traumatic event is in pieces and those pieces need to be put back together. We see this in the book of Job as Job wrestles with his experience and tries to understand what has happened to him. He engages in schema testing, exploring different explanatory schemas, trying to find the one that will work. This is when a survivor needs trusted listeners who can be there to listen, support, and validate their experience. This can only be done when we recognize the individuality of the survivor and honor their voice. We cannot lump survivors together and whip out a foolproof checklist for them to follow. We support a survivor when we honor the uniqueness of their experience and allow them to articulate it in their own way.

One of my favorite stories in the New Testament is when Jesus heals the woman with the issue of blood. This woman had been suffering for years. She had been taken advantage of by doctors, shunned by her community, and lost everything. Her trauma, and I think it's fair to call it that, left her alone, isolated, and without support. Her bleeding made her unclean and therefore unwelcome in religious spaces. She couldn't be touched because her uncleanness would spread to the other person. Just as Job was alone in his sickness, this woman was alone in her suffering. Until she met Jesus. She had no doubt heard of his power and his healings. And even though it was forbidden, she pushed her way through the crowd to get close to him. She believed that if she could just touch the edge of his garment she would be healed.

Notice how many of those things were uncalled for, forbidden, inappropriate. She shouldn't have been in the crowd; anyone she bumped into would be made unclean. She shouldn't be reaching out to touch a man, she would make him unclean, and she definitely shouldn't be doing it in secret. Wrong. Wrong, wrong. She was doing everything wrong. Her desperation drove her beyond the limits of what was appropriate. Let's look at the text:

> As he went, the crowds pressed in on him. Now there was a woman who had been suffering from a flow of blood for twelve years, and though she had spent all she had on physicians, no one could cure her. She came up behind him and touched the fringe of his cloak, and immediately her flow of blood stopped. Then Jesus asked, "Who touched me?" When they all denied it, Peter said, "Master, the crowds are hemming you in and pressing against you." But Jesus said, "Someone touched me, for I noticed that power had gone out from me." When the woman realized that she could not remain hidden, she came trembling, and falling down before him, she declared in the presence of all the people why she had touched him and how she had been immediately healed. He said to her, "Daughter, your faith has made you well; go in peace." (Luke 8:42-48)

There is so much in these few verses. It is a stunning story of the way Jesus operated. First, he is already on his way to do something. The leader of the synagogue has begged Jesus to come to his house and heal his daughter. Jesus is going with the man when this story of the bleeding woman takes place. Jesus is about his business. He's in the midst of ministry. He is surrounded by crowds and yet he stops and takes notice of this one woman. The pressures and demands of ministry do not stop him from speaking to this one woman, one woman who, by the way, could have been a source of controversy. She was unclean, she had potentially made him unclean by touching him. Yet, he stops and sees her. He stops everything to talk to her.

Given the state of our world today, it is easy to rush past the hurting. We can become so preoccupied with growth, budgets, business plans, and productions that we walk right past the bleeding people in our churches. The pressure to reach more people, to grow our membership, to add more services, to build bigger buildings becomes a self-perpetuating machine that focuses on numbers and forgets that each number is a person. A person who has come to our church for a reason. A person who has a story to tell. Trauma is messy, it is time-consuming, it can be uncomfortable, so we move it down the list of priorities. Isn't it more important that we show visitors what a great place we've created? Isn't it more important that we make sure new people are comfortable and want to come back? Isn't it more important that we keep up our giving so we can keep up our activities? We have become business minded instead of church minded. We have become hostages to the desperation to grow, the pressure to be bigger. To keep up appearances and keep up momentum we expect the wounded and the hurting to heal and heal quickly.

So, many times we develop, intentionally or unintentionally, a policy, a procedure, and a checklist to be followed when it comes to suffering. You've heard of the Romans Road? Maybe we could call this the Forgiveness Road. We listen to the survivor's story and then give them the same answer we gave the last person and the person before that. The focus is often on getting them to forgive someone or something. Then ta-da, we're done. You've forgiven them, now you're healed, and let's never discuss it again. And if the person who inflicted the wound is a pastor or someone in leadership . . . well, that Forgiveness Road might become a Forgiveness Zipline. We might put the welfare, reputation, and influence of the organization ahead of the health of the survivor. It's better to lose one person than lose ninety-nine, right? We're playing the numbers games, but we're playing it backward.

Jesus stopped in the middle of the crowd to meet one bleeding woman. He left the ninety-nine to go find the one. Jesus showed us the value of the individual, the value and worth of each precious person. The book of Job does the same. The friends had lots of theological answers, lots of doctrine that sounded good, a checklist for Job to follow, but they failed to value Job as an individual. They wanted him to be a part of their theological institution and there was no room for nonconformity. They failed to recognize that a survivor needs their own voice. The survivor's experience is their own and it will not fit into any mold we try to shove it into. The first step we need to take is to commit to listening to the individual, recognizing the uniqueness of their story, and giving them a place where they can tell their story in their own way. Rehearsed answers and standard responses have no place in being a trusted witness. We need to be willing to listen to hear, not listening to reply. We listen to receive the survivor's story to give them a place to share their pain, not tell them how to fix it.

This second stage is also a time for mourning and grief. Trauma involves loss. It may be the loss of a loved one, the loss of a dream, the loss of a marriage, or something else entirely, but trauma also involves the loss of our sense of safety in the world. It involves the loss of our sense of agency and control. It involves the loss of our understanding of the world and our place in it. There will be grief that comes with this. Unfortunately, our society is uncomfortable with grief and mourning. The messiness of grief can be uncomfortable for those who witness it. We don't know what to say, so we say nothing. We don't know how to comfort, so we stay away. We can't make it better, so we don't even try. Instead, we stay on the sidelines and wait for the survivor to feel better. We wait for the storm to pass. We wait for it to be easier. Then when they show up again a few weeks or months later, we pretend like nothing has happened and expect them to carry on like before.

This discomfort with grief is often true in the church as well, which is sad because the Bible is full of grief. There is nothing unbiblical about grief and mourning, but we have convinced ourselves that church is only for praise reports and smiling faces. We often skip past the loss to get to the resurrection. Instead of sitting with the pain and honoring the tears, we acknowledge the loss and jump right to the silver lining. It's not wrong for us to remember the joy that is coming. It's not wrong of us to remember the redemption God has promised us. But between Good Friday and Easter Sunday, there was the silence of Saturday. The disciples sat with their grief. Before the resurrection there was mourning. We need to be okay with grief if we are to walk with a trauma survivor. In trauma processing there is no skipping ahead to the resurrection. There is a silent Saturday to walk through first.

WHAT DOES A PLACE TO TELL THEIR STORY LOOK LIKE?

- Focus on the individual as an individual. Even if you have seen the exact same situation before, each survivor will process the experience differently. There is no standard response or procedure for trauma. We must invest the time to understand the individual and to respond with care and compassion that meets them in their need.

- Listen without judgment. Survivors need the freedom to work through their experience, and their words may not always be pretty. Being a trusted listener involves listening without judgment or agenda. The survivor is the expert on their experience.

- Validate and affirm the survivor's words. The chaos and confusion of trauma can cause a survivor to question everything, even themselves. Honor a survivor's feelings and words. "It makes sense that you feel alone." Affirm what is true. "This is awful and it should not have happened to you." Acknowledge what feels true to them. "I don't think it's true that God hates you, but I understand why it might feel that way."

- Defeat shame with truth. These two phrases can have a huge impact on a trauma survivor: "I believe you," and "This wasn't

your fault." Memorize them and say them often. A survivor will
need to hear them more than once.

- Be patient. Healing from trauma is a lengthy process and it may
  involve multiple trips around the same issue. Repetition is
  common in trauma processing. Be prepared to listen and keep
  listening as the survivor tries to find the right way to express and
  understand their experience.

- Allow the grieving process to take as long as necessary. There is
  no shortcut to resolving trauma.

A Place to Belong

As much as I love the book of Job, there are times when I get stuck on
the epilogue. It doesn't always sit right with me, and I get a little an-
noyed. After the whirlwind, Job's community shows up. I love this, but
I also struggle with it. Why? Because where were they when Job was
alone on the ash heap? Where were they when he was scraping his
diseased skin with a broken piece of pottery? Where were they when
the stray dogs were licking his sores? We know from the text that Job
had been a respected man in the community. He would sit in the city
gate and the young men would listen to him. He was well-known and
esteemed. And yet, when he suffered unimaginable tragedy, this same
community left him alone. The friends who did sit with him, who
come from far away, turned on him, condemned him, and blamed
him for his suffering. What kind of community is that?

Then God shows up. God speaks from the whirlwind and com-
mends Job. God calls Job "my servant." The friends who condemned
him have to ask Job to intercede on their behalf. It is only after all of
this that Job's community comes back. So, sometimes that irritates me.
This community turned their backs on Job when he needed them
most and then they come back when they find out that God is on
Job's side. It seems a little self-serving, doesn't it? When the church

functions as a business whose primary concern is the bottom line and growth (budgets and butts, if I may), the business interest of "what will benefit us most" makes it nearly impossible to care for and shepherd God's people. Protecting and perpetuating the institution is what matters. It's heartbreaking and unbiblical.

The good news is Job's community returns to him and accepts him as a trauma survivor. It is sad that it took them so long to go to him, but, in the end, Job is able to reconnect with his community. This is Herman's third stage of healing. The survivor needs to be able to have a place in their community again. The survivor needs a place to belong. Not just a church they attend or a community they visit, but a place of genuine belonging and acceptance. We've seen how isolating trauma can be, but, as human beings, we are made for relationships. The church is not a business, it is a family of believers. We are meant to be a community. And while there are plenty of splits and disagreements within the beautiful, diverse, eclectic family of believers, we are one body. Community can help in the healing of trauma . . . or it can make it much, much worse. The way we, as a community, respond to trauma will have a significant impact on a survivor's healing process. We need to take this seriously.

The issue for us as a community of believers is how we create space for trauma survivors. Are we making room for them? Are we welcoming and embracing them even in the midst of their suffering? A place of belonging will probably look different in every local church, so the question we must ask ourselves is what that looks like in our church community. And, more importantly, what would it look like for this specific survivor? Just as every community will look different, every survivor will have different needs. What do they need from their community to feel welcome, included, and valuable?

One of the other things we need to be prepared to do is accept the survivor as a trauma survivor. While this event should not become their sole identity in the church, it is also important that we honor what they have been through. Job's community came to him and consoled him for what had happened to him. They didn't ignore it, they didn't wipe their brow and say, "Whew, glad that's over with." There was an acceptance of Job's experience as a part of the community. Job was a changed man, as we see in the naming of his daughters and his choice to give them inheritances along with his sons. Job cannot go back to the way things were, and his community accepts him with these changes. There is not, and never will be, one right way to heal from trauma. There are certain similarities and consistencies in trauma responses, and this enables us to identify the general needs a survivor will face. But one person's healing journey may not look like another person's journey. Trauma gives us, as the church, an opportunity to recognize the uniqueness of each individual and to meet them right where they are.

WHAT DOES A PLACE TO BELONG LOOK LIKE?

- The community has the potential to greatly help or greatly harm a survivor. It will require intentionality to support a survivor in their healing.

- We cannot leave all connections to the survivor. As the survivor's support community, we can take the initiative to reach out and check in on them. A simple text message with no pressure to reply, bringing a meal to them, a phone call—actions that remind the survivor that they are a valuable part of our community and that they have not been forgotten.

- Provide the survivor with opportunities for agency. Asking them to pray for someone, giving them a chance to serve on a volunteer team, asking them to write a get-well card for another church member, are all small steps that may help give the survivor a sense of control and positive impact on the world.

- Accept the survivor as a trauma survivor. While the trauma is not their identity, it has become a part of their story. Embrace them as a valued part of the community with every part of their story.

- If they choose to share their story or engage in a survivor mission, encourage and support their endeavors. Notice I said, "If *they* choose." Sharing their story publicly is a decision that can only be made by the survivor. It doesn't matter how powerful it is, how much good we think it can do, or who we think it can help, it must the survivor's choice. It is their story to tell, not ours.

Conclusion

These lists are not exhaustive, and there are countless other ways comforters can support trauma survivors. These are meant to be a starting place, not a checklist. What are the next steps your church can take to create a community that welcomes and supports survivors? What are things you are already doing well? Where have you noticed a potential gap in your ministry? Do you have an experience with a trauma survivor that went well or one that went poorly? What would it look like for your church to be known as a safe place for survivors, a community that provides hope and healing, a community that walks beside the hurting? These are all questions that we can think through before the need arises. We might never be fully prepared for trauma, but we can decide, in advance, that we will embrace survivors and give them a place to call home.

Lessons Learned

- Judith Herman lists three things a trauma survivor needs for healing: safety, remembrance and mourning, and reconnection with community.

- As a church community, we can provide trauma survivors with a place of sanctuary, a place to tell their story, and a place to belong.

- There is no one right way to heal from trauma. Survivors must be allowed to use their voice, tell their story, and create their own healing journey.

REFLECTION QUESTIONS

- When you look at your church community, whether you are a survivor or a comforter, does it provide a place of sanctuary, a place to tell their story, and a place to belong? What is your community doing well and what can be improved?

- What type of support and comfort do you wish you had received in your time of suffering?

- What lessons does the book of Job teach us about trauma, supporting survivors, and healing?

CONCLUSION

CAN YOU REMEMBER A TIME when someone reached out to help you? Maybe it was as simple as someone paying for your coffee or sending you a sweet card. Can you remember that act of unsolicited kindness? Someone who cared enough to step in when you needed help, even though they didn't know you, or you couldn't pay them back? That kind of compassion and kindness changes things. It's not hard to find examples of people being cruel to one another . . . just hop on social media for ten seconds and you'll drown in it . . . but to see people who reflect the love of God? That's something truly beautiful.

When we come alongside a trauma survivor, we have the opportunity to be that hand of kindness. We have the opportunity to speak the words they need to hear, to support them as they walk through the unimaginable. We have the opportunity to be a light in the darkest of days. And make no mistake, it *is* an opportunity. To be trusted with another person's story is a gift. To be trusted with their pain, that is also a gift. It won't always be easy, but it is a ministry that is sorely needed in the church. We, as the church, need to learn how to support survivors. We need to relearn how to put people ahead of platform, prestige, and paychecks. Trauma is an opportunity for the church, an opportunity for us to live the gospel, an opportunity for us to love the broken and the hurting with no thought of what's in it for us. It is an opportunity to reflect the love of Jesus.

In a world that is increasingly superficial, trauma calls us to the deep. There are no easy answers here, no quick fixes or checklists to fill out. Trauma asks us to walk into the fire and stand in the ashes, so the survivor won't be alone. There will be questions and challenges, frustrations and joys. It is not an easy task to walk beside survivors as they heal, but it is what the church is called to do. We don't give up on the wounded, we don't cast aside the hurting, and we don't cover for the abusive. Or maybe I should say . . . we shouldn't do those things. Many times, we, as the church, have failed. We have failed to love the broken, we have failed to carry the wounded, we have failed to support the struggling, and we have failed to hold the guilty accountable because we valued something else more.

The book of Job has shown us both healthy and destructive ways of responding to trauma survivors. Job's friends didn't wait to be called. They heard about Job's suffering, and they went to him. They met him in the ash heap and sat with him for seven days. They wept beside him and gave him the ministry of their presence. That is something to be commended. The gift of presence to someone who feels alone, abandoned, and isolated is not a cheap gift. It was only when Job began to speak that trouble arose between Job and his "comforters." His words challenged their beliefs. They couldn't accept Job's story because it threatened their theology. Instead of listening to their friend, they tried to correct him, to get him to agree with them. Job called them "miserable comforters" for a reason. The support and comfort Job needed was nowhere to be found. Even when a fourth friend shows up, Job receives more correction, more accusation, more shame, and more blame. It is God himself who meets Job in his suffering and speaks words that lead to healing. Job is able to pick up the shattered fragments of his world and make something new out of them. He is able to leave the ash heap and rejoin his community. In their arms he is finally accepted as a trauma survivor. He can tell his story without fear. He lives the rest of his life, changed by the trauma he has been through, but able to live with hope for the future. He has learned the hard way about the fragility of life and the vulnerability of humanity and so he provides for his daughters. The community that shunned him becomes the community that embraces him.

The book of Job can also be a message for trauma survivors. Trauma is not your fault. You are not to blame. Your healing journey is yours and yours alone. Job shows us that we can scream and cry and struggle and God will still be with us. When we feel alone, when nothing makes sense, God is still there holding everything together. We don't have to dress up and act like everything is alright. God saw it all and God knows what you've been through. Job cried out to God and God met Job in the ashes of his pain. In the worst moments of Job's life, God was there. When Job's friends failed him, when his community abandoned him, God showed up. If you are a trauma survivor, you are not alone. I pray that some of the information in this book has given you insights and understanding for what you're going through. I pray that it has given you hope. I pray that it has released you from guilt and shame and given you a voice. There is another side to this storm. Hold on, my friend. You will make it through.

Friends, let us become communities that embrace the hurting and stand with the wounded. Let us sit in the ashes with survivors because that it where Jesus would go. Let us be communities that welcome and value those who have been through trauma. Let us be men and women who do not run from the tears of others. There is ministry to be done, there is healing to be shared, and there is love to be lived if we are willing to do it.

BIBLIOGRAPHY

Andersen, Francis I. *Job: An Introduction and Commentary*. Downers Grove, IL: Inter-Varsity Press, 2008.

Anker, J. "Metaphors of Pain: The Use of Metaphors in Trauma Narrative with Reference to Fugitive Pieces." *Literator* 30, no. 2 (August 2009): 49-68.

Baldwin, Jennifer. *Trauma-Sensitive Theology: Thinking Theologically in the Era of Trauma*. Eugene, OR: Cascade Books, 2018.

Balentine, Samuel E. *Job*. Macon, GA: Smyth & Helwys, 2006.

———. "Legislating Divine Trauma." In *Bible Through the Lens of* Trauma, edited by Elizabeth Boase and Christopher Frechette, 161-76. Atlanta: SBL Press, 2016.

Boase, Elizabeth. "'Whispered in the Sound of Silence': Traumatising the Book of Jonah." *The Bible & Critical Theory* 12, no. 1 (2016): 4-22.

Borbely, Antal F. "A Psychoanalytic Concept of Metaphor." *The International Journal of Psycho-analysis* 79, no. 5 (1998): 923-36.

Briere, John and Catherine Scott. *Principles of Trauma Therapy: A Guide to Symptoms, Evaluation, and Treatment*. Thousand Oaks: Sage Publications, 2015.

Cataldo, Lisa M. "I Know That My Redeemer Lives: Relational Perspectives on Trauma, Dissociation, and Faith." *Pastoral Psychology* 62, no. 6 (December 2013): 791-804.

Cauchi, Joseph. "Ezekiel 21:1-22 as Trauma Literature." *Australian Biblical Review* 69 (2021): 15-22.

Claassens, L. Juliana M. *Writing and Reading to Survive: Biblical and Contemporary Trauma Narrative in Conversation*. Sheffield, UK: Sheffield Phoenix Press, 2020.

Clines, David J. A. *Job 1–20*. Grand Rapids, MI: HarperCollins Christian, 1989.

———. *Job 21–37*. Grand Rapids, MI: HarperCollins Christian Publishing, 2006.

———. *Job 38–42*. Grand Rapids, MI: HarperCollins Christian Publishing, 2011.

Dick, Michael Brennan. "Legal Metaphor in Job 31." *The Catholic Biblical Quarterly* 41, no. 1 (January 1979): 37-50.

Dickie, June Frances. "Lament as a Contributor to the Healing of Trauma: An Application of Poetry in the Form of Biblical Lament." *Pastoral Psychology* 68, no. 2 (April 2019): 145-56.

Focht, Caralie. "The Joseph Story: A Trauma-Informed Biblical Hermeneutic for Pastoral Care Providers." *Pastoral Psychology* 69, no. 3 (June 2020): 209-23.

Fox, Michael V. "God's Answer and Job's Response." *Biblica* 94, no. 1 (2013): 1-23.

———. "Job 38 and God's Rhetoric." *Semeia* 19 (1981): 53-61.

———. "The Meanings of the Book of Job." *Journal of Biblical Literature* 137, no. 1 (2018): 7-18.

Frechette, Christopher G. "The Old Testament as Controlled Substance: How Insights from Trauma Studies Reveal Healing Capacities in Potentially Harmful Texts." *Interpretation* 69, no. 1 (January 2015): 20-34.

Frost, Robert. *Selected Poems.* New York: Fall River Press, 2011.

Garber, David G, Jr. "'I Went in Bitterness': Theological Implications of a Trauma Theory in the Reading of Ezekiel." *Review & Expositor* 111, no. 4 (December 2014): 346-57.

Granofsky, Ronald. *The Trauma Novel: Contemporary Symbolic Depictions of Collective Disaster.* New York: Peter Lang Inc., 1995.

Gutiérrez, Gustavo. *On Job: God-Talk and the Suffering of the Innocent.* Maryknoll, NY: Orbis, 1996.

Hartley, John E. *The Book of Job.* Grand Rapids, MI: Eerdmans, 1988.

Hawley, Lance R. *Metaphor Competition in the Book of Job.* Göttingen: Vandenhoeck & Ruprecht, 2018.

Herman, Judith. *Trauma and Recovery: The Aftermath of Violence—from Domestic Abuse to Political Terror.* New York: Basic Books, 2015.

———. *Truth and Repair: How Trauma Survivors Envision Justice.* New York: Basic Books, 2023.

Janoff-Bulman, Ronnie. "Assumptive Worlds and the Stress of Traumatic Events: Applications of the Schema Construct." *Social Cognition* 7, no. 2 (1989): 113.

———. *Shattered Assumptions: Towards a New Psychology of Trauma.* New York: The Free Press, 1992.

Janzen, David. "Claimed and Unclaimed Experience: Problematic Readings of Trauma in the Hebrew Bible." *Biblical Interpretation* 27, no. 2 (2019): 163-85.

Janzen, J. Gerald. *At the Scent of Water: The Ground of Hope in the Book of Job.* Grand Rapids, MI: Eerdmans, 2009.

———. "Job's Oath." *Review & Expositor* 99, no. 4 (Fall 2002): 597-605.

Jones, Serene. *Trauma and Grace: Theology in a Ruptured World.* Louisville, KY: Westminster John Knox, 2019.

Kelle, Brad E. "Moral Injury and Biblical Studies: An Early Sampling of Research and Emerging Trends." *Currents in Biblical Research* 19, no. 2 (February 2021): 121-44.

Kynes, Bill, and Will Kynes. *Wrestling with Job: Defiant Faith in the Face of Suffering.* Downers Grove, IL: IVP Academic, 2022.

Langberg, Diane. *Suffering and the Heart of God: How Trauma Destroys and Christ Restores.* Greensboro, NC: New Growth Press, 2015.

Longman, Tremper. *Job.* Baker Commentary on the Old Testament Wisdom and Psalms. Grand Rapids, MI: Baker Academic, 2012.

Margulies, Zachary. "Oh That One Would Hear Me! The Dialogue of Job, Unanswered." *The Catholic Biblical Quarterly* 82, no. 4 (October 2020): 582-604.

McDonald, MaryCatherine. *Unbroken: The Trauma Response Is Never Wrong.* Boulder: CO: Sounds True, 2023.

McKnight, Scot, and Laura Barringer. *A Church Called Tov: Forming a Goodness Culture That Resists Abuses of Power and Promotes Healing.* Carol Stream, IL: Tyndale House, 2020.

Middleton, J. Richard. *Abraham's Silence: The Binding of Isaac, the Suffering of Job, and How to Talk Back to God.* Grand Rapids, MI: Baker Academic, 2021.

Newsom, Carol A. "The Book of Job." In *New Interpreters Bible.* Volume 4. Nashville: Abingdon, 1996.

——. *The Book of Job: A Contest of Moral Imaginations.* New York: Oxford University Press, 2003.

——. "The Book of Job as Polyphonic Text." *Journal for the Study of the Old Testament* 26, no. 3 (March 2002): 87-108.

Nouwen, Henri. *The Wounded Healer: Ministry in Contemporary Society.* New York: Doubleday Religion, 2010.

O'Connor, Kathleen M. *Jeremiah: Pain and Promise.* Minneapolis: Fortress Press, 2012.

——. *Job.* Collegeville, MN: Liturgical Press, 2012.

——. *Lamentations and the Tears of the World.* Maryknoll, NY: Orbis, 2002.

Ortlund, Eric. *Piercing Levithan: God's Defeat of Evil in the Book of Job.* Downers Grove, IL: InterVarsity Press, 2021.

Perdue, Leo G. *Wisdom in Revolt: Metaphorical Theology in the Book of Job.* Sheffield, UK: Sheffield Academic Press, 1991.

Pippin, Tina. "Job 42:1-6, 10-17." *Interpretation* 53, no. 3 (July 1999): 299-303.

Platt, David. *Something Needs to Change: A Call to Make Your Life Count in a World of Urgent Need.* Colorado Springs, CO: Multnomah, 2019.

Pohl, William C, IV. "Arresting God's Attention: The Rhetorical Intent and Strategies of Job 3." *Bulletin for Biblical Research* 28, no. 1 (2018): 1-19.

Porges, Stephen W., and Seth Porges. *Our Polyvagal World: How Safety and Trauma Change Us.* New York: W. W. Norton & Company, 2023.

Poser, Ruth. "No Words: The Book of Ezekiel as Trauma Literature and a Response to Exile." In *Bible Through the Lens of Trauma,* edited by Elizabeth Boase and Christopher Frechette, 27-48. Atlanta: SBL Press, 2016.

Rambo, Shelly. *Spirit and Trauma: A Theology of Remaining.* Louisville, KY: Westminster John Knox, 2010.

Seow, Choon-Leong. *Job 1–21: Interpretation and Commentary.* Grand Rapids, MI: Eerdmans, 2013.

Shields, Martin A. "The Ignorance of Job." *Australian Biblical Review* 68 (2020): 28-39.

——. "Malevolent or Mysterious? God's Character in the Prologue of Job." *Tyndale Bulletin* 61, no. 2 (2010): 255-70.

Van der Kolk, Bessel. *The Body Keeps the Score: Brain, Mind, and Body in the Healing of Trauma.* New York: Penguin, 2014.

Van der Kolk, Bessel, and Onno van der Hart. "The Intrusive Past: The Flexibility of Memory and the Engraving of Trauma." In *Trauma: Explorations in Memory*, edited by Cathy Caruth, 158-82. Baltimore: The Johns Hopkins University Press, 1995.

Walton, John H. *Job: The NIV Application Commentary*. Grand Rapids, MI: Zondervan, 2012.

Webb, Marcia. "The Book of Job: A Psychologist Takes a Whirlwind Tour." *Christian Scholar's Review* 44, no. 2 (Winter 2015): 155-74.

Whitehead, Anne. *Trauma Fiction*. Edinburgh: University of Edinburgh Press, 2004.

Wilkinson, Margaret. "Undoing Trauma: Contemporary Neuroscience; A Jungian Clinical Perspective." *The Journal of Analytical Psychology* 48, no. 2 (April 2003): 235-53.

Wolfers, David. *Deep Things Out of Darkness: The Book of Job Essays and a New English Translation*. Grand Rapids, MI: Eerdmans, 1995.

SCRIPTURE INDEX